W9-BLV-096

BASEBALL

HOW TO PLAY THE GAME

BASE

HOW TO PLAY THE GAME

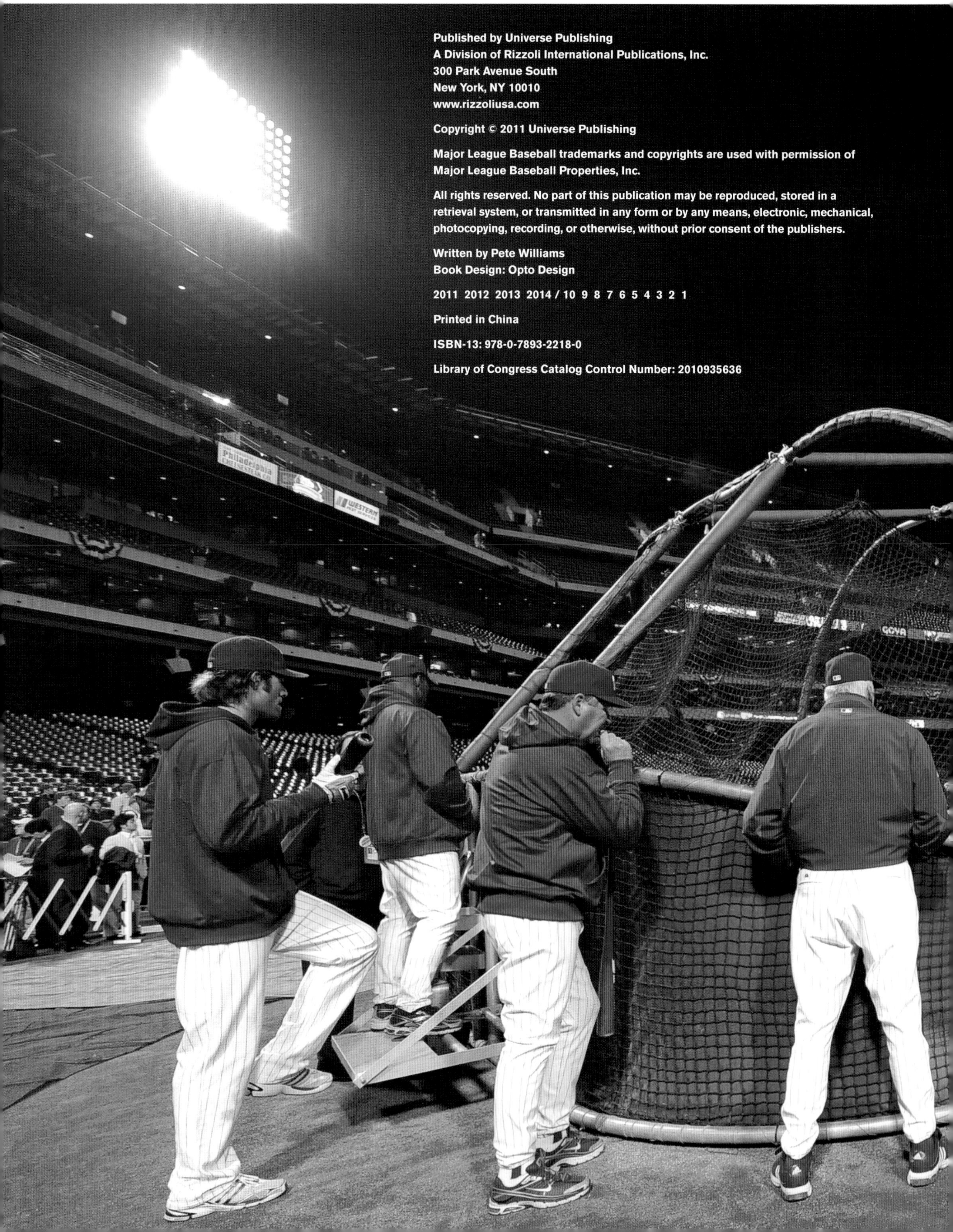

Published by Universe Publishing
A Division of Rizzoli International Publications, Inc.
300 Park Avenue South
New York, NY 10010
www.rizzoliusa.com

Copyright © 2011 Universe Publishing

Major League Baseball trademarks and copyrights are used with permission of
Major League Baseball Properties, Inc.

Written by Pete Williams
Book Design: Opto Design

2011 2012 2013 2014 / 10 9 8 7 6 5 4 3 2 1

Printed in China

ISBN-13: 978-0-7893-2218-0

Library of Congress Catalog Control Number: 2010935636

In addition to the diligent staffs of Major League Baseball's publishing division and Rizzoli Publications, we'd like to thank many people for their support on this venture. MLB's David James and the group at Harlem RBI, including Vince Coleman, Rebecca Muir and Robert Saltares, were extraordinarily helpful in giving this book the hands-on instructional photographs that you see. And we also could not have illustrated these instructional photographs without our models, including Basilio Garay, Roger Ramos, Jonathan Cruz and Steve Mullins. Likewise, Tim Maxey of MLB and the MLB Players Association, along with Nate Shaw of the Arizona Diamondbacks, were invaluable in their help and knowledge of conditioning.

Pete Williams has covered Major League Baseball for two decades for media outlets such as *USA Today*, *The New York Times*, *Fox Sports* and *SportsBusiness Journal*. He's the author or co-author of 16 books, including the MLB Insiders Club titles *Inside the World Series*, *Inside Spring Training*, *Baseball's Greatest Rookies* and *Baseball's Destinations*. He lives with his family in Safety Harbor, Fla.

MAJOR LEAGUE BASEBALL PROPERTIES

VICE PRESIDENT, PUBLISHING
Donald S. Hintze

EDITORIAL DIRECTOR
Mike McCormick

ART DIRECTOR
Faith Rittenberg

ASSOCIATE EDITOR
Jon Schwartz

SENIOR PUBLISHING COORDINATOR
Anamika Panchoo

PROJECT ASSISTANT EDITORS
Allison Duffy, Jake Schwartzstein

EDITORIAL INTERN
Daria Del Colliano

MAJOR LEAGUE BASEBALL PHOTOS

DIRECTOR
Rich Pilling

PHOTO EDITOR
Jessica Foster

PHOTOS ASSISTANT
Kasey Ciborowski

Harold Reynolds

Baseball is all about the fundamentals. We so often want to focus on the super play or the superstar, and although that can be good at times, what makes a great ballplayer and what makes this game great is the player who consistently makes the routine play. The guy who catches the ball, makes the right choices, throws to the right bases and runs out the routine ground balls — that's also the player who makes it to the Major Leagues. Don't get me wrong — everybody should aspire to be the best, even the All-Star player and the superstar. And yes, they, too, make the routine plays. I often hear that it's not always the best player who is the hardest worker. Don't be deceived — greatness comes with great sacrifice and extra work.

During my playing career, I encountered many great players and learned valuable lessons from each one of them. Players like Ken Griffey Jr., my teammate for several years with the Seattle Mariners, used to arrive at the ballpark early every day to take extra swings. Tony Gwynn, one of the greatest hitters I have ever been around, had a Hall of Fame career that included eight batting titles because he used to take extra batting practice every day — regardless of how well he was hitting at the time. Now, it's not only hitting that makes great players. I watched for years as Omar Vizquel challenged every coach to hit him a ground ball that he couldn't handle. If they were successful, he would buy them dinner; let's just say there were a lot of hungry coaches along the way. Great players like that put in the extra work. You may not see it, but they're always trying to better themselves. That's the attitude required to achieve greatness; great players are not going to be outworked.

I've always been big on executing the fundamentals because I was a small kid. I always had to do everything fundamentally correct in order to compete with other players who may have been more physically gifted. Much of what I learned about fundamental baseball was instilled in me when I was in youth baseball. When I was about

6 years old, I had a coach named Scott Laswell, who would make us run every time we took a third strike. He would say, "Swing the bat. Don't let the umpire call you out." I was always ready to hit, and that lesson stayed with me for my entire career. As a result, I was one of the toughest batters to strike out in the Big Leagues.

Young players often ask me what steps to take to become a Big League ballplayer. I usually answer that with a question of my own. The question I pose to those who tell me that they want to play baseball is, "Are you willing to do the little, simple, fundamental things and not be too flashy?" It might be cool to make a diving play and roll over to throw the ball, but chances like that don't present themselves every day. Don't focus so much on being a star; execute the fundamentals, and you'll stand out. Practice makes perfect, and perfect practice makes star players! When you're practicing, don't necessarily always go out and have someone hit you ground balls as hard as he can. Instead, have him roll ground balls to let you develop confidence and work on the fundamentals.

Along with proper fielding technique and the right approach at the plate, a good attitude is also a key to success. Your attitude will determine how far you will go in the sport. How many kids play youth baseball? Last I heard, there were several million — that's a big number. If I'm a college coach or a professional scout and I have that many kids to pick from, why would I put up with a kid who has a bad attitude? That said, with the proper fundamentals and the right attitude, maybe someday I'll be watching *you* play in the World Series!

Harold Reynolds, who played in the Big Leagues for 12 seasons and was a two-time All-Star, is currently a studio analyst for MLB Network. The *Harold Reynolds All-Star DVD Series*, featuring more than seven hours of instruction plus tips, drills and techniques from other All-Stars, can be found online at www.haroldreynolds.com.

Darrell Miller

Baseball is a sport in which the best players excel by virtue of a solid work ethic and a thoughtful approach to the game. Just as in life, there is no hiding in baseball. Not for long, at least. Each player in the field will have the ball hit in his direction. Each player on the basepaths will be forced to make a quick decision on a batted ball and then take an even quicker first step. Each pitcher will have to focus on his delivery and think about pitch selection to stay ahead of every batter. And each hitter will likely be called upon to face a dominant hurler or to advance a runner with the game on the line. When it is your turn in the batting order, you hit; there's no way to draw up a play for your team's biggest star when the game's outcome is hanging in the balance.

Perhaps more than any other sport, baseball is a game in which the fundamental skills are crucial at *every* level of the game. From Little League to the Majors, the game remains the same. Unlike basketball or football, in which size and strength can dictate drastic differences in strategy and style, fundamentally sound baseball is what separates champions from also-rans at every level of competition.

Each October, tense postseason games can be decided by a Big League player's ability to hit the cutoff man, drop down a key sacrifice bunt or stay in front of a hard groundball. The fundamentals that coaches and parents teach children make all the difference at the Major League level. Not only will the drills in these pages — artfully laid out in painstaking detail — hone the skills that will help players of every age and talent level each time that they take the field, but they will also foster a work ethic that will prove valuable beyond the diamond.

One of the special aspects of baseball is that it is meant to be played nearly every day during the season. The sport reinforces the work ethic and commitment needed to excel in school or employment while still managing to be a wonderful recreational activity that children can enjoy with their friends, siblings or parents. The best baseball instruction remains simple, fun and clearly connected to game action. Top-notch instruction should then be reinforced with impactful drills that challenge players both mentally and physically. And the best baseball instruction is in this book. With 18 chapters devoted to every aspect of the game — from equipment and pitching command to coaching tips and outfield defense — and advice from experienced coaches and bona fide Major League stars, past and present, *Baseball: How to Play the Game* provides the methods and the message needed to bring out the best in any player.

I am convinced that we have to take the opportunity to influence youth in our world with the values and character traits that baseball naturally teaches. We can use baseball to teach our youth the lessons that occur between the lines, and encourage them to take these lessons of everyday life with them outside of the lines.

A Major Leaguer for parts of five seasons, Darrell Miller has served as the director of MLB's Urban Youth Academy since its inception in 2006. For more Urban Youth Academy information, visit mlb.com's community page.

BASIC
FUNDAM

Approaching the game

ENTALS

"A GOOD FRIEND OF MINE USED TO SAY, 'THIS IS A VERY SIMPLE GAME. YOU THROW THE BALL, YOU CATCH THE BALL, YOU HIT THE BALL. SOMETIMES YOU WIN, SOMETIMES YOU LOSE, SOMETIMES IT RAINS.' THINK ABOUT THAT FOR A WHILE."
—Tim Robbins as Nuke LaLoosh in *Bull Durham*

Baseball really *is* that simple, at least in theory. If you can master the three essential elements of the sport — throwing, fielding and hitting — you're well on your way to becoming an excellent ballplayer. But it takes practice.

Where should you begin? A good approach starts with having a positive attitude and recognizing that baseball is a challenging game — a lot more challenging than Nuke LaLoosh makes it seem. Good hitters fail seven out of 10 times. Pitchers surrender home runs and must endure the indignity of a triumphant batter circling the bases. A player who boots a ball in the field feels all alone out there.

Players in other sports don't endure slumps the way baseball players do. A top running back will still rush for 50 yards on an off day and a star shooting guard will still connect for eight or 10 points even when he can't quite find his groove. In baseball, though, an 0-for-4 day at the plate is a common occurrence. Some days the ball just does not elude the defense, but on other days a batter might swear he's incapable of hitting the curveball — or even a batting practice fastball.

Although baseball is a team game, it's also a series of one-on-one match-ups and individual plays. That makes errors all the more pronounced, but it also magnifies the need for players to pick each other up and maintain positive attitudes at all times. For kids just learning the game, attitude can be an issue. After all, nobody likes to struggle, and it's tough to get a handle on baseball — literally at times. The basics of the game — catching a small white ball, throwing it where you want and hitting it with a long, round, tube-shaped stick — are more difficult than the entry-level skill requirements of most sports.

That's why it's important to learn the fundamentals first. Throw the ball, catch the ball, hit the ball. It's as simple as that.

Throwing

Kevin Kouzmanoff makes
sure to get a good grip on the
ball before throwing across
the diamond.

No matter what position you play, proper throwing mechanics remain the same. The key is to create momentum behind your throw and aim toward your target.

Most kids learn the game by playing catch in the backyard. Even though picking up a ball and throwing it might seem as natural to a youngster as hurling a rock or a snowball, it's important to learn proper throwing mechanics.

GRIP

The ball should be gripped by placing your index and middle fingers across the wide seams. Hold the ball with the inside edge of your thumb on the opposite side. There should be a little space between your index and middle fingers. Your ring finger and pinkie should be tucked on the side of the ball. Your index and middle fingers should be wrapped over the top of the ball, holding it with equal pressure from the base of your fingers to the tips. Don't hold the ball with a white-knuckle grip. Instead, keep a firm but relaxed grip on the ball.

BALL TRANSFER

Learning to get a quick, correct, consistent grip on the ball is important, because you're eventually going to have to make a speedy transition from fielding the ball to throwing it. You want the process to be simple and natural so that you do not have to spend a lot of time thinking about it. One way to practice this is by throwing the ball up in the air a few feet. Catch it, take it out of your glove with the proper grip and be ready to throw. (You don't need to actually make the throw for the purpose of this exercise.)

The more you practice this, the less you'll have to think about getting the proper grip on the ball out of the glove. That means you'll be able to make the throw faster, as well as make stronger, more accurate throws.

THROWING ANGLE

Get a good angle on your throw. Since you're just dealing with catch in the backyard at this point, aim square in the chest of your partner. Look at your target. Baseball is a game of hand-eye coordination, and it's tough to make accurate throws without maintaining eye contact.

To throw, get in an athletic stance with your feet positioned

Proper throwing grip

shoulder-width apart and your knees slightly bent. Your weight should be on the balls of your feet, with the foot of your throwing-hand side slightly behind your body. Shift the shoulder of your non-throwing arm in the direction you want to throw. Bring the ball back while bending the knee of your throwing-hand side as you shift your weight to your back foot.

Stride toward the target – your catch partner – by pushing off your back foot. Bring your throwing arm up and forward, keeping your elbow a little higher than your shoulder. Snap your wrist as you release the ball. As you follow through, bring your back foot forward and your hand and body around so that you finish square with the target.

Catching

Chest-level

Since throws can come from any angle, practice turning your glove to match the ball's location and making the catch at different heights.

We'll talk more about proper glove fitting later. For now, it's important to know that you should use a comfortable glove that's the right size for you.

READY POSITION

To catch the ball, start again in the athletic position with your feet shoulder-width apart and knees slightly bent, placing your weight on the balls of your feet. The foot of your throwing side should be slightly behind your body.

Put your glove out as if you're extending your arm to shake someone's hand. (If you're right-handed, think of it in terms of shaking someone's hand lefty.) If the ball is below your waist, you'll catch it with your fingers pointing down. If the ball is above your waist, catch with your fingers pointing up. If the ball is above or below your waist but thrown to the opposite side of your glove hand, catch it with your fingers pointing horizontally. Be sure to keep your eyes on the ball as it comes into your mitt.

When the ball strikes your mitt, squeeze it in your glove; then quickly reach for the ball and get a proper grip. Make a good throw back to your partner.

PRACTICE CATCHING FROM EVERY ANGLE

When playing catch, don't practice only chest-level throws. Have your partner throw you some pop-ups, too. The mechanics of catching a pop-up are the same. Keep your throwing-side foot slightly behind your body. Watch the ball all the way into your glove and catch it with both hands; your throwing hand should cover the glove after the ball is inside to ensure that it doesn't pop out.

LONG-TOSS

A great way to work on your throwing and catching is by playing long-toss, a drill that's popular at every level, including the Majors. In long-toss, you and your partner spend a few minutes throwing at a normal distance,

Below the waist

Above the waist

gradually backing up until you can no longer make the throw comfortably and with the proper mechanics. Younger players can keep the distance between them relatively short.

The idea of long-toss is to strengthen your arm and master long-distance throws. If you can throw at a longer distance, you'll be more accurate on shorter throws, as well.

Curt Schilling, who won World Series titles as a pitcher for the Arizona Diamondbacks and Boston Red Sox, attributes his power on the mound to playing long-toss as a kid.

"I didn't pitch until I was 18," Schilling says. "All my throwing came from third base, and those long throws across the diamond helped to build up my arm strength. A lot of it comes with physical maturation in addition to playing long-toss."

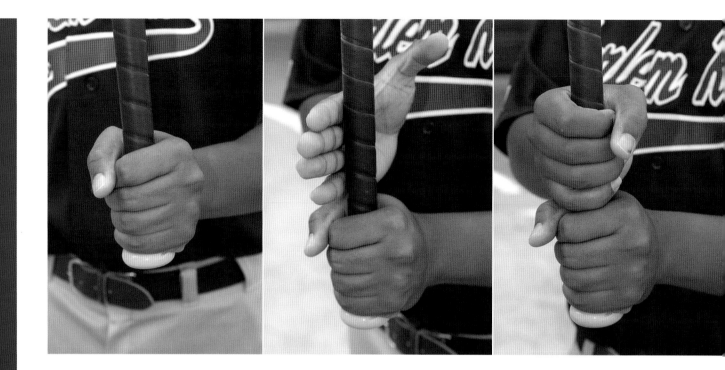

A proper batting stance begins with foot placement; your back foot should be parallel to the back line of the batter's box, with your front foot a little farther ahead of your front shoulder.

1

We'll talk more about hitting – including bat selection – later in this book. For now, let's assume that you have a bat that's the proper size – not too long or too heavy. Start by learning to hit from the side of the plate that coordinates to your throwing hand. Facing the pitcher's mound, a right-handed thrower will bat to the left of home plate and a left-handed thrower to the right. Switch-hitting is a skill that you can learn after you've mastered hitting from your dominant side.

HAND PLACEMENT

Wrap your bottom hand – the one nearest the pitcher, and the left hand in the case of a right-handed batter – around the bat just above the knob. Place your top hand above the bottom one and wrap your fingers around the bat in the opposite direction. Think of your grip as the bat resting in the part of your hand where your fingers meet your palm. Hold the bat firmly but with a relaxed, comfortable grip that allows you to swing easily.

FOOT PLACEMENT

When stepping into the batter's box, your back foot should be parallel with the back line and your front foot should be slightly beyond your front shoulder. Your knees should be slightly bent with your weight divided equally on each leg. Your front shoulder should be pointed at the pitcher, and you should turn your head slightly so that you're looking over your shoulder at the pitcher – or the tee if you're hitting off one – with both eyes.

Hitting

ON THE PITCH

As the pitcher winds up – or as you get ready to hit off a tee – transfer your weight to your back foot while moving your front foot forward a few inches. This is often referred to as the "wait and weight" response, since you're shifting your weight as you wait for the pitch. Rotate your hips back, as if coiling your body. From this position, you're ready to uncoil your hips, hands and bat to strike the ball.

Keep your head down and watch the ball all the way, even if you take the pitch and it goes into the catcher's mitt. When you do attempt a swing, make sure you swing all the way through. Some players let go of the bat with the top hand after contact, but that's a matter of personal preference. If you make contact, don't look at where the ball is hit. Drop the bat and run hard to first.

Like Adam Jones, any good hitter knows that it's important to keep your head down and watch the ball as you take your swing.

CONDITION DRILLS

Learning the basics of physical fitness

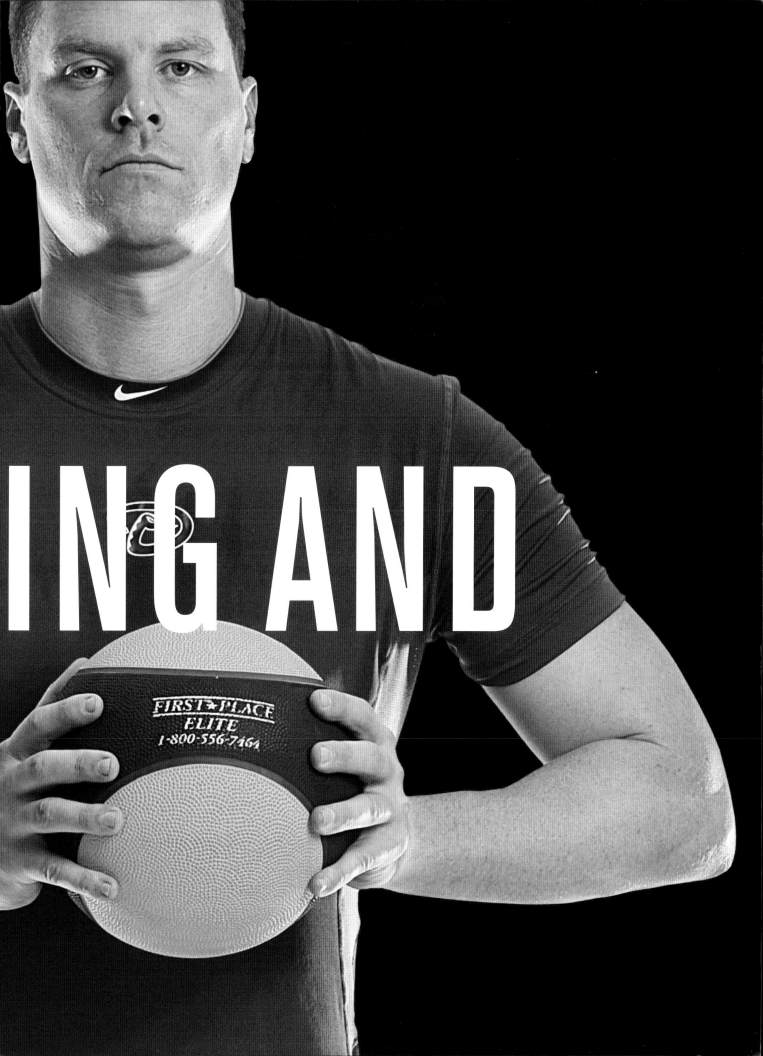

TRAINING FOR THE GAME OF baseball has evolved over the last decade to include muscle activation for preparation and weightlifting for strength. There are many choices to be made when it comes to exercise selection. The process is less than overwhelming if you consider a few simple concepts.

The game of baseball has some very specific requirements, some of which differ greatly from the requirements of many other sports. When considering a youth resistance training program, understand that the game of baseball can demand more of its players than other sports in a few categories. The ability of the player to move freely is key, as is shoulder development. It is very important that a young player can move and maintain control over his body weight prior to engaging in any loaded or weighted exercises. Correct form cannot be compromised to accommodate extra resistance.

Training to develop good posture is also very important. This allows the muscles of the shoulder blade, shoulder and hips to work optimally. Another key facet of a resistance training program for young ballplayers is that the exercises prescribed should be functional and involve as many joints as possible. For example, a lunge or a squat would be more beneficial overall than a bicep curl or leg extension because the former target multiple muscle groups. The reps for those exercises should fall somewhere between the 15–20 rep range per set. Keep these concepts in mind as you foster development among your team. They are, after all, the Major League players of tomorrow.

KEY CONCEPTS
- Warm up to stretch; don't stretch to warm up.
- Body weight before external resistance.
- Train for improved posture.
- Keep repetitions high.
- Never add weight at the expense of technique.
- Multi-joint exercises before single-extremity work.

Sumo Squat with Load Variations

Stand with your feet roughly shoulder-width apart and point your toes outward at a 45-degree angle. Pull your shoulder blades back, draw your belly button in and lift your torso upward so that you are standing upright with proper posture. Bend your knees and slowly lower them until the top portion of your thigh is parallel to the floor, as if you are sitting.

Pause, then slowly return to the starting position while making sure that your knees are pointing in the same direction as your toes throughout the movement. As you progress, add a dumbbell to the routine for resistance.

Stability Ball Hamstring Curls

Lay face up with your shoulders and hips on the ground and your feet on the stability ball. Lift your hips into the air and slowly pull the ball toward your body, then return the ball to its initial position. This motion targets your hamstrings and glutes.

Forward/Reverse Lunge Combo

Perform a forward lunge by stepping forward with one foot. From that position, leave your back foot planted and do a reverse lunge by taking a full step backward, thus making the back foot the front foot. Leg and hip strength, as well as stability, are the focal points of this exercise.

Double Leg Bridge

While laying face up, bend your knees and lift your butt up from the ground so that your shoulder, hip and knee are collinear. The double leg bridge targets both glute and hamstring strength, while also improving core stability and control.

Side Lunge

Take a large step directly to the side while keeping your landing heel in contact with the ground. Move your butt as close to the ground as possible, then return to a standing position. This lunge movement targets hip, groin and leg strength, as well as balance and control.

BOT

Dumbbell Row

Select an appropriately-weighted dumbbell and place your hand not holding the weight and your corresponding knee on a bench for optimum stabilization. Your foot that's in contact with the ground should be comfortably distanced from the bench for stabilization. Stabilize your abdominal muscles and retract your shoulder blade. Bring the dumbbell away from the floor by lifting your elbow toward the ceiling. The dumbbell should finish beside your torso. Such a motion targets abdominal stabilization with an emphasis on back and arm strength.

Push-Ups

Place your hands comfortably shoulder-width apart with only your toes and hands in contact with the ground. Your shoulder, hip and ankle should be collinear. Protract your shoulder blades, then lower your body to the ground and return to the protracted start position. These push-ups target your chest, core and the muscles around your ribs.

Bent-Over Tubing Lat Pulls

Stand with your feet shoulder-width apart and flexed to 90 degrees at the hip. Place the resistance belt anchored high and in front of you. Use one or two hands to pull your elbow toward your hip. This drill targets arm and back strength.

Foam Roll Dead Bugs

While lying longitudinally on a foam roll with a properly inflated, ribs-down position, maintain oblique tension and alternate heel touches. Add in a contralateral hand as you progress.

Planks (Front and Side)

Lying face down on the ground, raise your body into a plank position of stability so that only your toes, elbows, forearms and hands are in contact with the ground. The object is to keep your body as straight as a plank, avoiding a "sway" back or a high rear end position. Hold the plank for 10 seconds to start, progressively increasing the amount of time. The side plank can be performed in similar fashion, with the foot and forearm of one side of your body bearing your weight.

Medicine Ball Rotations

Standing with your feet shoulder-width apart and your elbows abducted, hold the medicine ball directly on your sternum. Rotate your torso using all available motion, alternating from left to right. Such movement is intended to target your abdominal and oblique muscles.

Shoulder Tubing T's, Y's, M's, ER@90 and ER@0Deg

These five exercises target your rotator cuff and the surrounding "throwing musculature."

1. Y's: Standing with resistance securely anchored at mid-chest height for all exercises, bring the shoulder tube handles away from the resistance, over your head and up into a Y shape.

2. T's: Bring both arms away from the resistance at shoulder height with your elbows straight.

3. M's: Extend your shoulders down until they are even with your body. Your hand should be positioned about 12 inches out to the sides away from your body.

4. ER@90: With your shoulders abducted to a 90-degree angle, flex your elbow to 90 degrees and externally rotate against resistance.

5. ER@0: Place a towel or something similar between your upper arm and thorax. With your arm by your side, flex your elbow to 90 degrees and externally rotate against resistance.

BASEBALL DRILLS
by Alex Rodriguez

PLAY CATCH

Sometimes I throw a tennis ball or racquetball against a wall and catch it with my bare hands. You can also try this on a handball court or anywhere else with a good wall. Try catching the ball with two hands and then with one hand. Don't think of it as work — make a game of it. You should take it seriously, of course, but you'll get better results if it remains fun.

KNEE DRILL

One drill I do that Hall of Fame shortstop Ozzie Smith made famous is called the "knee drill." Get on your knees and catch ground balls, which forces you to concentrate on improving the softness of your hands.

FOCUS ON YOUR FEET

The first thing that you need to concentrate on, which I feel is the most overlooked aspect of fielding, is your feet. It sounds funny, but you field ground balls with your feet. They dictate everything else you do. You can have soft hands, but if your feet are constantly out of position, you're going to be off target and out of rhythm. Once your feet are in position, surround the ball and be aggressive going after it. It's always better to be too aggressive rather than too passive, especially during practice.

SOMETIMES IT'S LUCK

When you play third base, the ball gets to you so much quicker than at other positions. That's why a third baseman is going to make a lot of errors. Sometimes you end up being lucky. People will say to me after I get to a hard-hit grounder, "Hey, great play." But I just got lucky.

EQUIP

Choosing the appropriate gear

MENT

BASEBALL PLAYERS ARE A NOTORIOUSLY superstitious bunch, especially when it comes to their equipment. Even at the Major League level, where players have a virtually unlimited supply of bats, gloves, hats and other equipment necessities at their disposal, they will stick with one item if they believe it's the source of a hot streak or high performance.

Can you blame them? A good glove becomes an extension of a player's body, as dependable as a trusted friend. Wooden bats have become disposable — thus the use of cost-effective aluminum by non-professionals — but a Big Leaguer will always bemoan the loss of a broken bat that had provided him a few days' or weeks' worth of hits.

Even if you're not a Big Leaguer, you can appreciate the value of comfortable equipment. The game is difficult enough without the added worry of breaking in a glove, wearing ill-fitting shoes or trying to find a batting helmet that feels natural.

Baseball might not seem like an equipment-laden sport when compared to the excess gear used in football, ice hockey or lacrosse, but the game requires a pretty big equipment bag even for just the essential items — let alone accessories such as sweatbands, sunglasses and sunflower seeds.

It's possible to keep costs down by purchasing used equipment, provided that it's in good condition. The term "gently used" is usually an oxymoron when it comes to youth sports, but sometimes you can find gloves and cleats that were barely worn because they were not a good fit for their original owner.

Baseball equipment, though universal in function, is a matter of feel and preference. One player's discards can be another's treasure. Regardless of choice, the top two priorities when choosing equipment should always be safety and comfort.

CHOOSING THE RIGHT BAT
by Ryan Howard

DON'T OVERESTIMATE YOUR STRENGTH

You have to select a bat that works for you. It's not true that the bigger the bat, the farther you'll hit the ball; it's basically how *you* work the bat. One thing that I was told is that if you can take a bat and hold it in front of you with your arm straight out and the bat pointing away from you, then it's probably a good size for you. But if you try to hold it up and you're having trouble keeping it steady, then it's too heavy. You have to make sure it's something that you can control.

EMULATE, DON'T IMITATE

I used to emulate Ken Griffey Jr. He was my idol; he was my guy. It's always good to try to emulate somebody to get a basis but, at the same time, to fold it to your mold, because there's only one Ken Griffey Jr. As much as you can imitate him, you can't *be* him. You have to kind of take what works for you and mix it into your own style and your own flair.

LOOSEN UP

Don't focus on swinging hard. For you young hitters, the key is that it's a game of opposites. The looser you are, the looser your hands are; the more relaxed you are at the plate, the quicker your swing will be. When you try to kill the ball, the first thing that happens is you will get tight. The tighter you are, the harder you'll try to swing and the slower your swing is going to be, the longer your swing is going to be, so the ball probably won't go as far. A lot of hitting is about being loose. It's an opposites type of approach. If you want to hit the ball hard, the approach is to relax — the opposite of what you think it is.

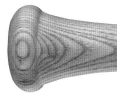

At the professional level, in which wooden bats are used, players put a great deal of time and effort into selecting their lumber. They are meticulous about hardness, length, weight, the distance between wood grains and several other factors that affect the makeup of a bat. Out of a shipment of two dozen bats, only five or six will usually make the cut to be used in games. The others will be used for batting practice or autographed and given away.

ALUMINUM VS. WOOD

Because wooden bats break frequently, they're cost-prohibitive at the youth, high school and college levels. Amateurs usually need only worry about selecting aluminum bats. Although baseball purists dislike metal and the "ping" sound the bats produce, aluminum has many advantages beyond cost. The hitter can generate more bat speed swinging the lighter, hollow aluminum bat, and thus can hit the ball harder and farther.

AGE APPROPRIATE

As with gloves, young players will grow out of their bats. Parents should not buy a larger bat with the mindset that the child will grow into it. He will, but he'll have a hard time hitting until he does. Youth leagues and high school associations also have regulations about weight, barrel size and length-to-weight ratio. It may be tempting to splurge on a high-tech aluminum bat that can cost hundreds of dollars, but many can be had for less than $50.

Bats

Glove Story

Outfielder

Catcher

First Baseman

Before 1950, many Big League players spent their entire careers using just one or two gloves, preferring to have an old glove restitched rather than purchasing and breaking in a new one. Even when they did buy new gloves, these players tended to keep their old ones as souvenirs. Why mess with success?

AGE APPROPRIATE

Little has changed since then, although most players now receive a steady supply of new gloves through their contracts with manufacturers.

Of course, Big Leaguers no longer deal with hands that are still growing. A 7-year-old will not be using the same glove when he's 14. Because it's possible for a 14-year-old to use the same glove into adulthood, though, it's a better investment to buy a higher-end model at *that* point. Parents should avoid purchasing a larger glove for a younger player thinking that the child will grow into it. He will, but in the meantime he'll struggle to field balls — and possibly risk injury — by wielding a glove that's too big for his body.

POSITION APPROPRIATE

Most kids in Little League try every position, so it's hard to go wrong with a youth outfield glove. But as you get older, the size and style of a glove is determined by position. Pitchers and middle infielders wear smaller gloves than outfielders and third basemen. First basemen and catchers have specifically-styled mitts. Many outfielders and third basemen prefer gloves with open webs that better enable them to see balls into the mitt. Middle infielders sometimes go with open webs, but the style is not recommended for pitchers, who use the closed webbing to better hide their pitches.

BREAKING IN A GLOVE

There are numerous ways to break in a new glove, but the goals are always the same: Soften the leather and form the pocket in the glove. To soften the leather, use modest amounts of glove oil or shaving cream. Spread the cream or oil evenly around the glove; don't pour it on.

The easiest way to form the pocket is by playing a lot of catch. This is the fastest and most fun way to break in a glove — but sometimes it's not fast enough. When you're not playing, place a baseball in the pocket of the glove and tie it shut to help hasten the process.

Keep your glove in a cool, dry place when it's not in use. You don't want the leather to dry out, so avoid car trunks and attics. Avoid getting the glove wet, too. If it does get wet, wipe it with a towel and let it air dry.

Batting gloves help you to get a better grip on the bat and lessen the sting of a ball that strikes the bat the wrong way. The gloves also protect your hands while hitting and running and prevent painful cuts, scrapes and blisters.

Like every other piece of baseball equipment, it's important that your batting gloves are comfortable and fit well. You want the gloves to be snug but not to eliminate your feel for the bat.

When you shop for batting gloves at a sporting goods store, try them on before buying them. And make sure to walk over to the bat section to test how a bat feels in your gloved hands.

Batting gloves are not just for batting. Runners wear them on the basepaths to protect their hands when they slide, while some fielders don them under their fielding gloves to lessen the sting of sharply hit balls.

Batting Gloves

Every time you go to the plate, you should be wearing a properly sized batting helmet. Getting hit in the head by an errant fastball, even at the Little League level, can cause significant damage without a helmet.

A helmet with double ear flaps offers the best insurance against injury. The helmet should be snug but not so tight that it gives you a headache. When you move your head from side to side, the helmet should not shift around. The helmet should consist of a hard outer shell with a firm layer of foam on the interior.

Coaches and players serving as coaches at first base and third base also should wear batting helmets as a precaution while on the field. Lightweight plastic batting helmets, like the ones given away as promotions at the ballpark, obviously should never be worn for protection.

Batting Helmet

Players ages 8 and younger can get away with wearing a good pair of sneakers to play baseball, assuming that the soles of their shoes provide plenty of traction. For everyone else, it's best to go with a pair of cleats.

SIZE

The most important features of baseball shoes are proper fit and support. Kids go through a lot of shoes, both on and off the field, but, again, this is no time to embrace the philosophy that a child will grow into a larger pair. Shoes that don't fit correctly will be uncomfortable and leave the athlete more susceptible to injury. Because shoes stretch with use, choose a pair that fits snugly when you first wear them.

SPIKES

Older players wear cleats so that they have better traction in the batter's box and on the basepaths. Metal cleats provide better traction than rubber ones, but, since metal cleats can be dangerous when a runner slides into an opposing player, many youth leagues don't allow them.

Limit your use of cleats to the field. They're not practical for walking and can damage floors and car interiors, not to mention that hard surfaces will wear down the actual spikes themselves.

Cleats

A catcher wears more gear than the other eight players on the field combined. That's because he puts himself in danger with every pitch. A foul tip or wild pitch has the potential to cause the catcher serious harm. But good equipment goes a long way toward preventing injury.

An athletic supporter and protective cup are the most important pieces of equipment, for obvious reasons. The catcher wears a mask and helmet to protect his face and head. The hockey-style helmet-mask was popularized by Big League catchers in the late 1990s and is a good alternative to traditional masks but can be expensive. The chest protector should cover not just your chest, but your groin area with a flap, as well. It also should cover your throat. Shin guards should cover your kneecaps fully in the squat position and should shield as much of your toes as possible.

Catcher's Gear

Hitting is a challenging enough task without combating sweaty hands on a hot day. Sweatbands worn on the wrists can help. Plus, they look cool – just ask former Big League outfielder Dusty Baker, who has continued to wear them as a manager long after his playing days ended. Be sure to wash your sweatbands regularly.

Sweatbands

Alex Rodriguez

Uniforms

Different players like their uniforms to fit in different ways. Double-knit fabric is flexible, so a uniform can be worn snugly. Some well-conditioned players, like Hall of Famer Dennis Eckersley, Alex Rodriguez and former Big League outfielder Ron Gant, like to wear their pants tight. Others, like Manny Ramirez, prefer a looser look. Uniforms should not be so tight that they restrict movement. Conversely, some argue that baggy uniforms are less aerodynamic.

When it comes to the length of baseball pants, preference again plays a role. Some players prefer pants that stop at the calf, while others like theirs to go to the heel. Some youth leagues mandate how pants should be worn, so keep that in mind.

Ultimately, most youth players have little input into their assigned uniforms. After all, wearing a uniform is not about *individual* expression. The top priority is performance, so find a uniform that fits well.

Sunglasses

Sunglasses aren't just for looks. They shield your eyes from the sun's harmful rays and also help fielders corral balls otherwise obscured by the sun's glare. There are numerous companies that make affordable shades designed specifically for baseball; normal fashion sunglasses aren't made for sports and might come off while you're running.

Many baseball sunglasses feature lenses designed to eliminate glare and enhance vision, especially when the sun is bright. So-called amber sunglasses are popular among ballplayers, although the lenses actually are gray or brown.

Stretching and Support

If you have a chance to get to a Big League game early, you'll likely see players on their backs with ropes or bands wrapped around their feet to stretch out their legs. So-called active-isolated stretching (AIS), popularized by kinesiotherapist Aaron Mattes, is different from conventional stretch-and-hold routines. Instead of holding a stretch for 10 to 30 seconds, the idea behind AIS is to hold the stretch for just two seconds, exhaling as you do so. This can reprogram the range of motion of your muscles.

You don't need to spend a lot of money for bands. Go to a home improvement store and have them cut a six-foot length of rope (for kids) or an eight-foot length (for high school and adult players). It should cost less than $5 and is a great way to stretch out before a game or practice.

An athletic supporter and protective cup are not just necessary for catchers and pitchers. No matter where you are playing on the field – even the outfield – there's the potential for injury. It takes just one sharply hit ball to do serious damage. Even younger male players need to protect their sensitive groin region by wearing both an athletic supporter and a protective cup at all times on the field.

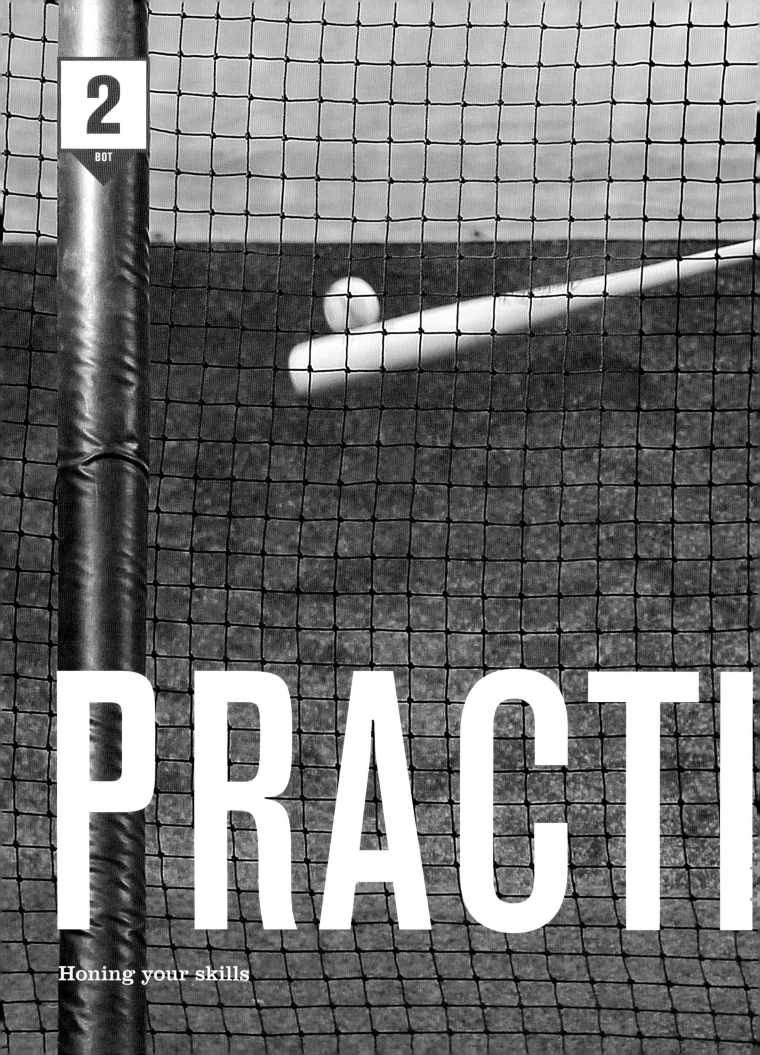

PRACTI

Honing your skills

IN HIS BEST-SELLING BOOK *OUTLIERS*, Malcolm Gladwell suggests that success is less a product of talent and natural ability than it is a result of experience. He cites examples from business, academia and sports to demonstrate how a number of successful people spent 10,000 hours or more honing skills for their respective crafts in childhood and young adulthood.

Baseball, more than most sports, requires a mastery of finely tuned, specialized movements. Unlike football and basketball, in which size is more of a factor, it's difficult to find examples of prominent baseball stars who took up the game in their teenage years simply because of a physical predisposition to the sport. Instead, most baseball players begin to play in early childhood and rack up 10,000 hours or so of practice by the time they reach adulthood. That's an average of 20 hours a week from the ages of 8 to 18.

Baseball is replete with examples of players who ate, drank and slept the sport as kids. Ted Williams obsessed over becoming "the greatest hitter who ever lived." Mike Piazza camped out in his backyard batting cage, developing the hitting stroke that enabled him to go from a 62nd-round draft pick to the best hitting catcher ever. Star closer Billy Wagner threw for hours against a barn growing up in rural Virginia.

Many stars from Latin America filled their days with little more than school and baseball. Others, such as Ken Griffey Jr., Cal Ripken Jr. and Barry Bonds, grew up with fathers who played or coached professionally. And then there are those Japanese players who typically learn the game in a baseball culture where practicing for four hours a day — including 90 minutes of conditioning — is not uncommon.

Of the many routes to becoming a great baseball player, all involve hours of practice. "We played seven days a week when we were younger," says former Seattle Mariners slugger Jay Buhner.

Like pick-up basketball and backyard football, sandlot baseball is mostly a relic of the past. These days, most kids don't play baseball informally. Nearly all play is organized into leagues, teams and schedules. That's not necessarily a bad thing. But if a player's development is solely a product of an organized structure, it's imperative that coaches make the most of that time.

Practice How You Play

Legendary football coach Vince Lombardi once said, "Practice does not make perfect. Only perfect practice makes perfect."

Most coaches prefer a less hard-line stance, opting for a philosophy along the lines of "practice how you play." The idea is that the way you practice determines how you will perform in the game. That's true in terms of execution and effort. Some players believe there's one speed for practice and a different one for games. But it's difficult to suddenly turn up the effort when you've generally approached the game with less intensity.

The same is true with mechanics. If you practice fielding, throwing or hitting with a lackadaisical approach, you'll do things incorrectly in games. The worst thing you can do is practice something incorrectly for hours over the course of weeks or months. All you've done then is developed a bad habit and reinforced it with repetition. That's why it's important to learn how to do things correctly the first time and to reinforce the positive through practice.

PRACTICE
by Mark Teixeira

TAKE IT SERIOUSLY

You're not going to get better if you're just joking around with your friends during practice. It's important to take a lot of ground balls — even more than you might think are necessary. And remember: Always concentrate!

BE PREPARED

The first thing you should learn is how to field bunts and weak hits. As a first baseman, you're going to be put in a lot of situations in which you and the pitcher need to communicate. You need to know who's going where at all times. Every time a ball is put in play, there is a chance it will be thrown to first base. You must always pay attention to the situation, be prepared to receive the ball from a teammate and know what to do after you catch it.

TARGET PRACTICE

It's important to master the most crucial part of the job: You need to be a good target. That's the big thing. Make sure that you're giving the infielders a good target. Also, work on your scoops. Work on picking the ball out of the dirt so that it becomes second nature.

Game day is exciting, but practice is when kids learn the strategies they need to excel on the playing field, as well as the value of discipline and hard work. Since players spend more time practicing than playing games, it's important that they enjoy the process and that coaches make it fun – or at least fast-paced.

MULTIPLE STATIONS

The popular image of a baseball practice is of 12 or so kids fidgeting in the field as they wait their turn to rotate to the plate for some batting practice swings at pitches thrown by a coach. If a kid believes that playing baseball is boring, it might be because he's too frequently been subjected to such a practice. But practices at the college and professional levels are anything but leisurely, stand-around affairs.

If you get to a Major League game early enough for batting practice, you'll notice that there's a lot more going on than just hitting in the cage. There are screens set up around the infield and a pair of coaches hitting fungos to infielders from either side of the cage. There's another screen in shallow center field where another coach with a fungo bat will be hitting to the outfielders. There's probably yet another coach sitting on a five-gallon bucket in foul territory and soft-tossing baseballs to a player hitting into a net.

Most youth and high school programs do not have protective screens, vast coaching staffs and a grounds crew to move all of the practice essentials back and forth.

Still, this same basic approach can be taken.

SEEK ASSISTANCE

Youth teams typically have one coach and one assistant. Parent volunteers can be a big help. A meeting at the start of the year with parents – before the one with players – can go a long way toward getting that help. Such gatherings also open the lines of communication that can thwart some of the parent-coach drama that all too often becomes a part of youth sports.

After explaining your philosophies and expectations to the parents, ask for volunteers who wouldn't mind occasionally attending practice and helping with drills. Stress that you're not looking for additional permanent

Keep Practice Moving

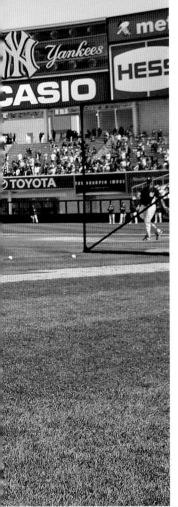

assistants, just more manpower to help get the most out of practice sessions for your players.

BE ORGANIZED

At the college and professional levels, coaches map out practices to the minute. This might seem unnecessary at the youth level, but it does force you to approach the day with a plan. If you have an organized practice, you'll likely keep the players active, engaged and enthused.

Practice often begins with two lines of kids playing catch to warm up. Once everyone has arrived – stress the importance of being punctual from day one – it's time for some stretching, but not so much as to bore players. They come to practice eager to play, and the last thing you want to do as a coach is dull that enthusiasm with too much conditioning.

After stretching, one way to get the blood pumping is to have the team run the bases. This reinforces what the players have learned about baserunning, and it's also fun. When they're done, gather the players around to catch their breath while you set the goals and agenda for the day.

Once the housekeeping is over, break the players into small groups. With a typical 12- or 16-player team, this translates into three or four groups. Assign one group to a hitting drill, another to a fielding drill and another to throwing or baserunning. The goal is to keep everyone active and engaged and to avoid the typical batting practice rotation that leaves many players standing around. One way to organize practice is to start by hitting fungos to the infielders and outfielders. This requires the help of two coaches. From there, transition to working on cutoffs and relays, with some players as baserunners, and then move on to baserunning drills.

Players look forward to batting practice – arguably the most important drill – which is why it should be saved for last. A player only gets a few chances to hit each game, and that's not nearly enough swings to master a skill that's one of the most difficult in all of sports.

Rotate the players through four batting stations in groups of three. The first is live hitting, batting against the coach or parent-volunteer. L-screens are inexpensive and enable the batting practice pitcher to throw at a close range to the batter without worrying about being struck by sharply hit balls. Have those hitters alternate, taking eight or 10 swings at a time. A second group can be behind the backstop playing soft-toss or hitting against a tee.

During soft-toss, a coach, parent-volunteer or another player tosses the ball from the side or from behind a net. The batter swings into a net – soft-toss nets are inexpensive – or simply stands in front of a fence and hits the ball into it. He also can hit from a tee into the fence, with a coach or teammate continually feeding balls to the tee. (We explain hitting from a tee and soft-toss more in the chapter "Hitting: Approach" and in the drills section at the back of the book.)

That leaves two or three other groups that can rotate to shag balls in the outfield. There will also be pitchers and catchers working on the side, requiring the supervision of another coach or parent-volunteer. Again, it is useful to have extra help.

No matter how active and engaging your practice, it should be age appropriate. Kids ages 8 and under will struggle to last more than one hour. As they get older, their attention spans lengthen, and they have a broader knowledge of the game. Baseball is more mentally draining than physically demanding, so keep that in mind when scheduling the length and nature of a practice.

With the 8-and-under group, it helps to change drills and stations often and to put an emphasis on baserunning. There's a reason that some professional teams allow kids onto the field after Sunday afternoon games to run the bases – it's a blast.

These days, kids seem to have as many games as they do practices, sometimes even more, since they're often involved with multiple teams. The key is to make sure there's adequate time for practice, both during the week and before games. It's very beneficial to take kids to a professional game early to see how the pros essentially pack a two-hour practice into their pregame session.

You won't be able to emulate a Big League routine, of course. Sometimes your game field might not be available until 30 minutes before the first pitch. But many of your drills can be done off to the side, especially if you have some portable nets for soft-toss or hitting off a tee.

KEEP A HEALTHY DIET

During those initial meetings with parents and players, make a point to stress the importance of nutrition. Baseball might not be as physically demanding as other sports, but it takes just as much mental focus, if not more. That's tough to maintain on an empty stomach. These days, with both parents working in many families, it's a challenge just to get the kids to practice, let alone feed them beforehand. Suggest easy grab-and-go options like fruit, a bag of nuts or trail mix, or an all-natural energy bar. Encourage kids to drink water. Sports drinks were designed for football players and endurance athletes sweating profusely in the summer heat. Such beverages are okay in moderation for baseball players,

but drinking lots of water before, during and after practice should be part of any young athlete's strategy. Once kids make the connection between how they fuel their bodies before practice and games and their subsequent performance, they'll make nutrition a part of their game plans.

GET OUT AND PLAY

Practice need not be boring. To do anything at a high level requires lots of practice. Alex Rodriguez, though physically blessed, attributes his success to practicing for countless hours at the Boys & Girls Club in Miami. "The key was playing all the time and performing certain drills over and over," Rodriguez says.

Above all else, stress to players that playing should not end after practice. Just as a piano teacher expects pupils to rehearse between lessons, it's important that players are active between organized practices. If they truly love the sport, kids won't find this a chore, and they'll be well on their way to accumulating more than 10,000 hours of experience.

"I remember going to the park a lot with my dad and spending a lot of time fielding grounders and hitting," says Craig Biggio, the former Houston Astros star. "Any time I could play, I did. If you're having fun and playing a lot, you're going to get better."

Soft-toss

PITCHING: MECHA

Learning different grips, types of pitches and deliveries

WHEN IT COMES TO PITCHING, there's nothing more important than proper mechanics. They can make the difference between a dominant pitcher and an ineffective one. Mechanics often determine whether a pitcher will be durable or frequently injured.

What makes teaching mechanics so challenging, though, is that there's no one-size-fits-all method. Leo Mazzone, the pitching coach for the great Atlanta Braves staffs of the 1990s — headlined by Cy Young winners Greg Maddux, Tom Glavine and John Smoltz — notes, "You don't try to clone pitchers."

In the early '90s, the Braves' rotation featured a pair of left-handers: Glavine and Steve Avery. Glavine stood on the third-base side of the rubber, even though most lefties stand on the first-base side. The third-base side provided a better angle for Glavine, who painted the corners of the plate with one of the game's best change-ups and a sinking fastball.

Avery, a power pitcher with a high-90s fastball and a nasty curveball, took the more traditional approach, standing on the first-base side of the rubber, which gave him a better angle to approach the hitter.

While some pitchers with textbook mechanics have difficulty getting the ball over the plate consistently, others take unconventional, yet effective approaches that leave pitching coaches scratching their heads in amazement. Indeed, each decade seems to produce a Major League phenomenon with a whirling delivery — take Fernando Valenzuela, Hideo Nomo or Dontrelle Willis, to name a few.

Many coaches won't tinker with an effective pitcher, no matter how unusual his approach might seem. But even within the fluid field of pitching mechanics, there are certain universal guidelines that young players should follow.

The key element of pitching mechanics is that they feel natural. "You can't concentrate on mechanics while you're pitching," says Hall of Fame hurler Tom Seaver. "You should be doing things automatically."

Get a Grip

The fastball is a pitcher's most important weapon. It provides the foundation for everything else he does on the mound. It doesn't matter if a pitcher's fastball maxes out in the low-80s or hits triple digits — the ability to throw it for strikes is the key to success.

Young hurlers must first master the grips of the four-seam and two-seam fastballs — in that order — before trying more advanced pitches. The four-seam fastball, as the name suggests, is held across the "horseshoe," or the two widest seams of the ball. The grip is the basis for other pitches and teaches young pitchers how spin affects the ball's movement. It also provides for maximum velocity on the ball. All four seams should create a perfect backspin on the ball, giving it a better lift.

FOUR-SEAM FASTBALL

On a four-seam grip, your fingertips should have contact with the seams, and your thumb should be under the ball. Your fingers should be a comfortable distance apart but not too far — the farther they're spread, the less velocity on the throw. Your thumb should be below, acting as the anchor.

Younger players with small hands might be more comfortable initially gripping the ball with three fingers — index, middle and ring — until their hands are big enough to master the grip with just their index and middle fingers. Either way, your fingers — whether two or three — should go across the seams.

The four-seam fastball consists of a gentle grip and an easy release. Don't choke the ball. The throw will stay straight, which is why infielders use a four-seam grip to throw. As pitchers develop, they will experience some natural movement on their four-seamers.

TWO-SEAM FASTBALL

Unlike the four-seam fastball, which is held across the seams, the two-seam fastball is held *with* the seams. For both grips, it's important to have your fingertips rest on the stitches, not on the slick part of the ball. Holding the stitches enables you to pull on the ball, creating friction and backspin. The faster the ball spins, the more it will move.

With a four-seam fastball, more spin means more power in the pitch. With a two-seam grip, spin equals movement. Grip the ball with the seams either on top or with your fingers across the narrowest seams. Pressure on your index or middle finger at the release point will produce added movement. Because of the finger pressure, though, velocity decreases. The key is to maintain consistent arm action and arm speed so as not to tip the pitch.

Sliders and sinkers can be thrown from the two-seam grip when the ball is held off-center. Generally, a power pitcher is going to stick with a four-seam fastball, while pitchers with less hum on their heaters will work more from the two-seam grip.

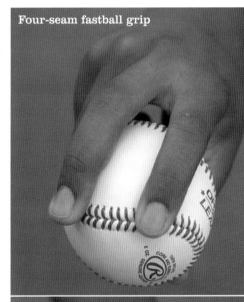

Four-seam fastball grip

Two-seam fastball grip

Curveball grip

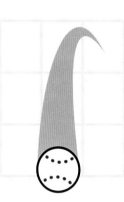

After you have mastered both types of fastballs, it's time to add off-speed pitches to your arsenal. But when exactly should you find ways to bolster your repertoire? That's open to debate.

INJURY RISK

A generation ago, pitching injuries from overuse were not nearly as common – nor diagnosed – among young players as they are today. With one-sport specialization becoming the norm, though, baseball is a year-round endeavor. That, combined with many parents placing their kids on a pre-professional track at a young age, has contributed to more overuse injuries, especially among pitchers.

In 1998, Dr. James Andrews, a prominent sports surgeon in Birmingham, Ala., performed elbow ligament replacement (Tommy John) surgery on just five patients who were of high school age or younger. In 2008, he did the operation on 28 kids in that age bracket. So many youngsters

have injured their arms throwing curves and sliders in recent years that doctors now refer to the trauma around the growth plates as "Little Leaguer's elbow." According to David Zeman, an orthopedist in Phoenix who works for the Arizona Diamondbacks, the ligaments and growth plates of the elbow don't mature sufficiently until ages 13 to 15.

"There are just too many people out there who don't know how to teach a breaking ball," says Tom Glavine, who used mostly a fastball and one of the game's best change-ups to win 305 career games. "Kids are running the risk of getting hurt. Rather than learning how to throw a curveball or another pitch, focus on just trying to throw your fastball for strikes."

John, who won more than 160 games after undergoing the pioneering reconstructive elbow surgery in 1974 that now bears his name, believes that throwing a curve is no more dangerous than throwing a fastball – if the

youngster has proper instruction and has developed physically.

But, John says, "Kids who are 10 or 12 years old just aren't strong enough. If a curveball is thrown properly, then there's little danger of hurting your arm. But you have to be strong enough to get over the top of the ball so that you can get your hand in the right position to throw it. For that, you need to be at least 15 or 16, when you have the proper strength and coordination."

CURVEBALL

To throw a curve, hold the ball along the long seam to allow four seams to hit the wind while the ball is in flight, producing movement. Curveballs typically are thrown with the middle finger along the length of the outside seam. The ball is held farther back in the hand than it is on a fastball, so the thumb also applies pressure along the entire length of the ball, not just at the tip. The curve should be thrown from the same arm position as the fastball.

Arsenal

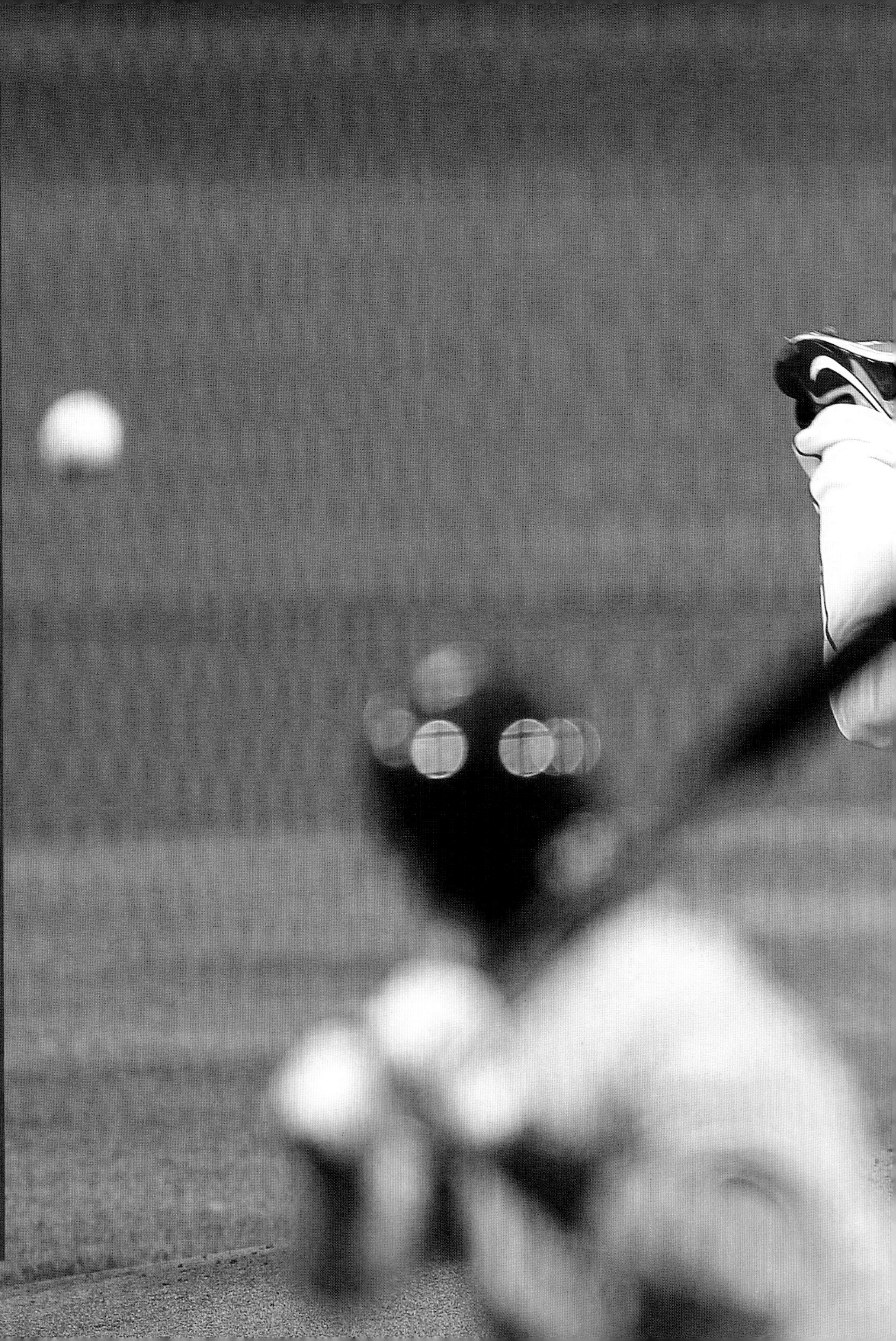

THROWING
by John Lackey

STRENGTHEN YOUR ARM

I think that one of the best ways to throw harder and build arm strength is by playing long-toss. Stretch your arm out, and gradually work up to throwing the ball as far as you can. Try to keep the ball on a straight line, and don't throw so far that it arcs high in the air or hurts your shoulder. You really need to work on your arm strength, which will help you down the road.

STICK WITH WHAT WORKS

The biggest key to my success has been trying not to change too much. I've taken what worked in Triple-A and carried it over to the Big Leagues. I had to make some adjustments, but I mainly try to stick with my strengths.

LOCATION, LOCATION, LOCATION

I like to talk to kids about having a purpose. A lot of kids just throw the ball; they don't really aim it at a target. When I was little, I had a target on the wall in the garage that I used to throw at. It's important to really concentrate on location every time you throw the ball rather than just pick it up and chuck it.

Slider grip

SLIDER

The slider is a cousin of the curveball, but it moves more like a fastball, which makes it a highly deceptive weapon.

One distinct advantage the slider has over the curve is that it's easier to learn, though there's much less vertical break. But the pitch places even more strain on the elbow than the curve, and, for this reason, it's a pitch that should be attempted only by hurlers who have struggled for a long period of time to develop an effective curveball – they likely will find it easier to master.

The slider is a fastball cut in the opposite direction of a sinker. The slider has a number of popular grips, but the most important thing to remember is that your middle finger acts as a pressure point.

Baseball coaches are quick to stress that even those players who can master breaking pitches at a young age should use them very sparingly. The key is to use your early years to develop arm strength by throwing mostly fastballs. Focusing on breaking balls could cost a pitcher velocity as he gets older.

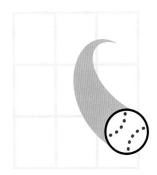

Jamie Moyer

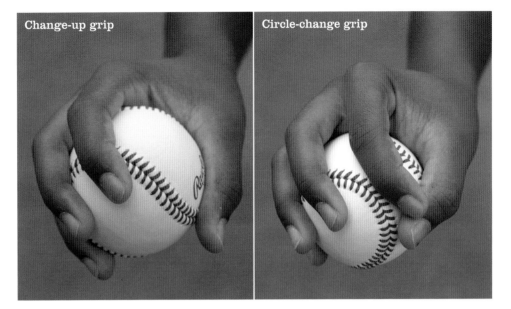

Change-up grip

Circle-change grip

CHANGE-UP

"Kids are so anxious to try what they see on TV, and the neat pitches are breaking balls," says Tom Glavine. "But most Major Leaguers who have good fastballs and breaking balls will tell you they wish they had a change-up. The guys who are successful have good fastballs and change-ups. It's a lot easier to learn to throw a change-up than a curve."

The change-up is a safer pitch for youngsters to throw than a slider or a curve, and it's an effective one, as well. It's an off-speed pitch that's eight to 10 mph slower than the fastball, carrying little more velocity than a batting practice fastball. But it's delivered with the same arm speed and action as a fastball, so the batter starts his swing early, reducing his power.

Since the pitches are delivered with the same approach, the key difference is in the grip, which changes the speed. The change-up is thrown with the same arm speed as the fastball, but the ball is released off the second row of knuckles rather than the fingertips. The hand is behind the ball.

CIRCLE-CHANGE

A circle-change is one of the more popular change-ups. It's gripped with the index finger tucked against the thumb. The ring and middle fingers are along the seams. The ball slides off those fingers, with the force directed alongside the ball, which takes something off the pitch.

With a four-seam circle-change, the two middle fingers are across the four seams. The

thumb and index finger touch to form a circle on the side of the ball. This pitch produces more backspin than others. It looks like a four-seam fastball but is slower.

Many pitchers, such as the ageless Jamie Moyer, enjoyed long careers with little more than an effective change-up to complement a mid-80s fastball; they keep batters off balance by constantly changing the speeds of their pitches.

Curt Schilling, one of the greatest postseason pitchers of all time, didn't even attempt to throw a curveball until he was 18 years old and did not throw one in the Major Leagues.

"You don't need a curve to get people out," Schilling says. "You need to change speeds. If you can master the change-up, you'll be just as effective, if not more."

DELIVERY
by Jason Marquis

GET IN THE RIGHT FRAME OF MIND

First of all, good control starts before you step onto the field. Hard work and determination are the most important things to start with. Also, listen to your coaches and other people who know what they're talking about.

KEEP YOUR DELIVERY CONSISTENT

Pay attention to your arm slot as you practice pitching. The arm slot is the angle your arm is at above your head when you're about to deliver the ball. It should remain the same on every pitch.

TRAIN YOUR ARM

It sounds obvious, but you need to put in the practice on the mound. Work on your mechanics, and when you find a good pitching motion that works for you consistently, repeat the same mechanics over and over again until they become second nature. Finally, don't just stand out there and throw to your catcher. When your catcher is giving you a target, don't just aim at it, either. Instead, try to throw the ball *through* his glove at that spot. With hard work and an approach like that, pitching with control will come a lot easier for you.

A pitching delivery need not be as complicated as it looks. Each pitcher's delivery can be broken down into three distinct stages: from his initial stance to the balance position; from the balance position to the stride foot's landing; and after his stride foot is down on the mound.

Begin in a comfortable athletic stance, with your hands relaxed and both feet on the rubber. Starting with the ball in your glove is recommended, since it prevents tipping pitches to the opposing batter. Take a small step back – a large step could cause you to lose balance – and bring your arms over your head to begin your wind-up. Turn on your right foot (if you're a right-hander) and plant it in front of the rubber to help you drive toward home. Lift your left leg up while turning your hip until your left leg and hip are square with the rubber.

Next, bring your left leg down and your right hand out of the glove. Your arm should come up to the overhand position (or arm slot) as you move forward with your stride. Bend your landing leg. Release the pitch out over your front leg (your left leg if you're a righty). After your release, bring your back (right) leg around to propel your body forward. Shift your weight toward home plate.

Momentum is going to carry a right-handed pitcher toward first base and a left-hander toward third. Pitchers naturally want to finish in an ideal fielding position, but oftentimes that's not possible. Better for you to focus on your delivery and mechanics and rely on your infielders to make the plays behind you than to try to stop your momentum off the mound and risk injury in the interests of better defense.

Delivery

A pitcher's delivery can be
divided into several stages:
the balanced athletic
position; the transition into
the stride; and the completion
of the stride.

By working on your
mechanics and repeating a
smooth delivery in practice,
like Mariano Rivera does, you
will become more effective in
game situations.

PITCHING: COMM

Understanding how to best work the full strike zone

ONCE A PITCHER HAS DEVELOPED working mechanics and delivery and has established an effective fastball, it's time for him to work on his command.

Pitching command and pitching control are often used interchangeably, but the terms refer to two different concepts. Control is simply the ability to throw a pitch for a strike, as opposed to out of the strike zone or to the backstop. Command is a pitcher's ability to do not only that, but also to target different sections of the strike zone. When a pitcher talks about his ability or inability to command pitches on a given outing, he's referring to how well he was able to pinpoint spots.

Command is a mastery of location. The most important ability for a pitcher is the ability to throw a two-seam and four-seam fastball frequently, using both sides of the plate. These pitches should be thrown in all four quadrants of the strike zone: up and in, down and in, up and away, and down and away. A pitcher who can do that will be effective regardless of the other pitches in his repertoire.

How important is a pitcher's command? Don Drysdale, the late Hall of Fame hurler for the Dodgers, liked to say that if "pitchers threw the ball exactly where they wanted to every time, hitters wouldn't hit .300 or even .250. Pitchers must use the entire plate to be successful."

The strike zone is generally defined as the area over home plate between the batter's armpits and the top of his knees. This real estate, of course, is a moving target depending on numerous factors — starting with the height of the batter. Some umpires have wider strike zones than others. Savvy catchers can influence an umpire's call by framing pitches. In the Majors, players frequently talk about how veteran pitchers or batters get the benefit of the doubt from umpires.

"You just try to be consistent," says Randy Marsh, who umpired in the Majors for 29 years before retiring prior to the 2010 season. "A pitcher might not like a certain pitch, but he knows it's going to be called the same way in the ninth inning as it was in the first. The hitters know it and the pitchers know it."

Tom Glavine and Greg Maddux, neither of whom had overpowering stuff, were perhaps the game's two best pitchers of the 1990s when it came to command. Glavine made a living by "painting the black," spotting his pitches on or around the black perimeter of home plate. Maddux, the four-time Cy Young Award winner, commanded his pitches so well that he made strikes look like balls and balls look like strikes.

Warren Spahn, the Hall of Fame left-hander who won 363 games, had his command down to a formula. "The secret of successful pitching is to be able to throw strikes — but to try not to whenever possible," he said. "The plate is 17 inches wide, but I always figured the middle 12 belonged to the hitter. The two-and-a-half inches on the inside and outside were mine."

A sudden lack of control can be caused by a mechanical flaw, but that's easily corrected by working with a pitching coach or simply by relaxing. As for command, that's something that only comes with practice.

Sandy Koufax

Taking Command

The first rule of pitching is to stay ahead of the hitter. Throw a first-pitch strike, and get the first batter out. Make him hit *your* pitch, not the one he wants.

To do this requires you to take command, and not just by pinpointing your pitches. The battle for the plate has been waged for as long as the game has been played. Batters crowd the plate, pitchers brush them off. It has become a bigger challenge for pitchers since the late '90s, when batters began coming to the dish wearing elbow padding and other body armor, unafraid of getting plunked. Brady Anderson, the former Baltimore Orioles outfielder, started the trend by wearing a Rollerblade elbow pad.

Sluggers like Barry Bonds, Andres Galarraga and Alex Rodriguez soon followed suit.

CLAIM THE PLATE

As a result, the plate-huggers could claim the inside part of the plate as their own, hoping pitchers would throw to the outside part of the dish, where hitters can fully extend their arms for optimal power. Or, by crowding the plate, the batter can manipulate the strike zone, creating the illusion that an inside pitch over the plate is a ball.

"I always felt that half of that plate was mine and half of it was the pitcher's," says former Astro Craig Biggio, who was plunked a record 285 times in his career.

Many players today interpret any inside pitch as something just short of attempted murder, unlike the players of a generation ago, who realized that such pitches were just a part of the game.

"The art of pitching is the art of instilling fear," Sandy Koufax once said, meaning that a pitcher cannot be afraid to claim the inside part of the plate or even the area between the inside of the plate and the batter.

"The inside fastball is the pitch that will establish the outside corner for you," Hall of Famer Tom Seaver wrote in his book *The Art of Pitching*. "The batter cannot dig in on you if he knows that you are willing to throw inside. Your fastball is the best way to establish that you are the boss and that he, the batter, must be on the defensive."

WORK THE ENTIRE PLATE

Once you have claimed that real estate, it's time to work all four quadrants – something that takes years of practice. Even Nolan Ryan, one of baseball's greatest pitchers, once struggled with his command. Early in his career with the Angels, Ryan led the American League in both strikeouts and walks six times.

As a pitcher, you want to avoid 2–0, 3–1 and 3–2 counts. The best way to do that is by establishing the fastball. Leo Mazzone, the pitching coach of the great Atlanta Braves staffs of the '90s, preached to his pitchers the importance of asserting the fastball early in the game and in the count. By doing that, you can force hitters to respect the fastball and swing, rather than to sit back and wait on the breaking ball.

It also conditions you to trust your fastball, throw it most of the time and reinforce your command. Mazzone stressed this formula for all of his pitchers, whether they were flamethrowers like John Smoltz or moundsmen like Greg Maddux and Tom Glavine, who capitalized on command and changing speeds.

"What makes the off-speed pitches so effective is when you can hit spots with your fastballs," Glavine said. "Whether you throw 85 or 95, if you can do that, a hitter has to respect it."

ATTACKING THE STRIKE ZONE
by Josh Johnson

DON'T BACK DOWN

Just go right after every batter, even the best ones. It's a great feeling to be the pitcher who goes after an opponent's big hitter and manages to get him out. If you give up a hit, well, he's been getting hits off everyone else, too, so no one will blame you for it. If he's the best hitter, then he's been hitting everyone around. But if you're fortunate enough to get him out, you'll be on cloud nine.

GO WITH THE FLOW

It's important to be calm, cool and collected. I grew up with my parents telling me that — just have fun. You're out there playing a game. It should be fun. It shouldn't be serious all the time. There are times when it can be serious, but when you're in Little League, you should just be playing hard and giving it your best shot. The more you do that, the better you become, the better the teams will be that you get to play on, and the more fun it will be when you win games and big tournaments.

SHAKE IT OFF

If someone hits a home run off you, it's over with — you can't go back in time and change it. You've got to go on and say, "Whatever happened, happened."Just get back on the mound and go after the next batter the same way.

Situational Pitching

PITCH 1: Fastball, low and away

PITCH 2: Fastball, high and inside

PITCH 3: Change-up, low and inside

Smart pitchers pay attention to the habits of batters and vice versa. But, at the youth level, players often don't see enough of any one opponent to pick up on patterns and trends.

THE COUNT

Starting a batter off with a fastball is always a good bet. Of course, hitters will be looking for the fastball, so it's important to throw it in or away, preferably at knee level. Come back with another fastball at letter height, which many batters will chase. An 0–2 count is the perfect time to drop a change-up. Because a change-up uses the same pitching motion as a fastball, the batter will be early with his swing.

Since batters look for fastballs on the first pitch, a breaking ball (if you have one) or even a change-up can be an effective option, too, as long as you throw it for a strike. The change-up is more effective if the batter has already seen your fastball earlier in the game.

The count will determine your approach. In his book *Nolan Ryan's Pitcher's Bible*, Ryan stresses to pitch a batter inside when you're ahead in the count and away when you're behind. If you're ahead in the count, the batter is going to protect the plate more, which is all the more reason to throw inside and jam him. If the batter is ahead in the count, it makes sense to nibble on the outside corner. If he makes good

contact, at least you've neutralized his power.

WITH MEN ON BASE

Many pitchers change their approaches dramatically with runners on base. This isn't a good idea, since it can lead to overthrowing and a loss of control. The same strategy of commanding your fastball, working the quadrants and changing speeds should be employed with runners on.

Don't surrender the strike zone just because there are runners on base, and don't let the runner become a distraction. Go with your best stuff, and try to limit the damage. A double-play ball with the bases loaded and no outs is a good tradeoff after allowing a hit. Keep your team in the game and learn from all of your experiences.

Mark Wohlers, the pitcher who surrendered the home run to Jim Leyritz that shifted the momentum of the 1996 World Series from the Atlanta Braves to the New York Yankees, was second-guessed for throwing a slider instead of his 100-mph fastball. Wohlers never regretted the pitch, only that he did not command it down and away as he had hoped.

"You determine what pitch you're going to throw, you believe in it and you throw it," Wohlers said later. "There's no second-guessing. I still feel like I threw the right pitch to Leyritz; it was simply in the wrong direction."

THE CHANGE-UP
by Tim Hudson

DON'T SLOW DOWN

One of the most important things about throwing a change-up is having the same arm speed as you do for your fastball. The other really important thing is to get out in front with it. Don't let your arm drag. Get out there and finish the pitch.

GET A GRIP

The thing that changes the pitch's speed is the grip. You can change grips. Some people throw a circle change-up, and some people split their fingers and throw more of a split-finger change-up. Just find a grip that's comfortable to you and is something that you can throw strikes with, but at the same time take velocity off.

NEVER STOP LEARNING

I was 21 when I learned the change-up. It's probably one of the easier pitches to learn and definitely the easiest off-speed pitch on your arm. If you throw a change-up correctly, it shouldn't hurt your arm.

When a runner reaches first base, you must take a different approach to the plate by operating out of the stretch position as opposed to the full wind-up. For right-handed pitchers, that means placing your right foot in front of and parallel to the rubber with your back toward first base. For lefties, it's the opposite. It's tougher for a runner to steal against a left-hander, since a lefty pitcher will be facing first base from the stretch.

The goal of the stretch position is to add speed and deception to your motion to keep the runner from stealing or getting a significant lead. That keeps the possibility of a double play alive.

After getting the sign from the catcher, you should be ready to come to the set position by shifting your body upright while bringing your throwing hand inside your glove – all in one motion. Your weight should be on the back leg, not leaning forward.

While in the set position, you can move only your head. Any movements with your shoulders, hands or legs will result in a balk. You may step off the rubber without balking, but, even then, you cannot split your hands until your rear foot is off the rubber.

One of the simplest weapons you have in the stretch position is the ability to hold the ball. Instead of the runner dictating the pace of the game, you remain in command when you're in the stretch. The runner might maximize his lead and then decide to inch back to first. He might get caught off balance or give away his intention to steal. The hitter, meanwhile, could be taken out of his rhythm and be forced to call a time out in the batter's box.

Such cat-and-mouse movements might not be the most exciting things for those in the stands to watch, but they're an integral part of baseball strategy. The key as a pitcher is to be unpredictable with runners on base. You don't want to provide a pattern to which a runner can adapt and steal.

Holding Runners on Base

PICK-OFF MOVE

Andy Pettitte has one of the greatest pick-off moves in the game's history. It helps that he's left-handed, but he also has worked at it. Pettitte stresses the importance of making sure that everything looks the same each time, regardless of whether you're throwing to first or going home.

"Your head is the most important thing," Pettitte says. "If you look at first base the whole time, they'll know what you're going to do. I look to home, but I make sure I can see the runner out of the corner of my eye."

A pitcher's concern over runners on base depends on the situation. With a lead of two or more runs with two outs and a runner on first, the threat of a steal is not a huge concern. If the runner steals second, it still takes at least one hit to drive him in, and he's not even the tying run. It's better to let that happen than to throw a bad pitch that gets hit out of the park.

Andy Pettitte

3
BOT

PITCHING: HEAT

Developing a wind-up that adds velocity

ARE POWER PITCHERS BORN OR MADE? The question has sparked an age-old baseball debate.

Some of the game's hardest throwing pitchers, after all, have been tall and imposing physical specimens on the mound — just take Walter "The Big Train" Johnson, Bob Gibson, Tom Seaver, Nolan Ryan, J.R. Richard, Roger Clemens and Randy Johnson as a few examples.

But many power pitchers also have been of average or below average build. Bob Feller stood just six feet tall on the mound. Pedro Martinez, Billy Wagner and Tim Lincecum threw pitches that approached 100 mph with builds in the 5-foot-10, 175-pound range, or smaller.

Feller attributed his strength and velocity to his work while growing up on a farm in Iowa, decades before strength training and physical conditioning would become the norm in baseball. Wagner, who grew up in rural southwestern Virginia, spent hours throwing a ball against a barn, in part to take out the frustrations of a hardscrabble childhood. But that repetition over thousands of pitches also reinforced his mechanics, creating a 5-foot-10 force who was ignored by college scouts but later developed into one of the game's greatest closers.

Then there's the rail-thin Lincecum, who worked with his father as a boy in his home state of Washington to develop an unorthodox yet highly effective delivery, producing velocity that would seem impossible coming from a young hurler with such an unassuming physique.

The 6-foot-4 Ryan threw gas from the start of his career with the New York Mets. But he was able to harness and sustain that speed on his pitches until age 46 by consistently adhering to a conditioning program that emphasized strength and flexibility in the legs, especially in the hips.

"You can't teach height," many basketball scouts say about the advantage held by 7-foot players. But pitching velocity can be learned. Like every other aspect of baseball, it is a physical gift for some; more often than not, though, it's a combination of four factors: mindset, repetition, mechanics and conditioning.

Nolan Ryan

Tim Lincecum

Billy Wagner

TOP
4

Pitching coaches from Little League to the Majors teach pitchers not to overthrow. Any attempt to go deeper into the well for a few extra miles per hour on the fastball – especially in a tough situation – can often lead to a loss of control, a bad pitch or even an injury.

But there's something to be said for adopting the mindset of a power pitcher on the mound. The momentum and confidence built from blowing gas past opposing hitters can fuel your adrenaline so that you throw just as hard at the end of the game as you did on your first pitch.

Curt Schilling, a career 11–2 pitcher in the postseason and a military aficionado, says that he thrived on the tension and strategic maneuvering of big-game situations: The pressure brought out his best velocity.

"As a power pitcher, you always feel like you're in charge and you're going to dictate what's going to happen, and when it doesn't go your way, you're surprised," Schilling says. "But there's a psychological element that has to exist in order to make things work. It all comes back to control of the situation. You know you're going to throw a fastball;

the batter knows it; the crowd knows it. You know he's not going to hit it, and so does he. There are times when you can just feel the outcome before it happens. That's what power is.

"Power pitchers don't exist in the Big Leagues just because they throw hard. They exist because they strike people out. It's an art, and it takes a lot of mental input. I always took pride in having command, both of my pitches and of the game situation. It's a puzzle you have to put together, and I think that's why there's always a mystique surrounding power pitchers."

Mindset

Curt Schilling

Tom Seaver

Repetition

If it seems like there are fewer power pitchers in the Major Leagues throwing high-90s gas today, it might not be a coincidence. Many coaches believe the early specialization that countless youngsters in baseball subscribe to these days puts them in a pre-professional mindset. Instead of focusing on perfecting their two-seam and four-seam fastballs, they start tinkering with off-speed pitches. Not only is this potentially dangerous, but it also threatens their ability to develop velocity.

Tom Seaver recalls receiving some valuable advice from a former Giants utility infielder named Ernie Bowman early in his Minor League career. Bowman wondered why Seaver wasn't using his heater more often in games. "Kid, you got a good fastball," he told Seaver, "but to keep it, you gotta throw it. Don't save it for Christmas."

Translation: When it comes to velocity, it's either use it or lose it.

PUSHING OFF
by Jaret Wright

GET SET

The basic set position starts with your back foot parallel to and just in front of the rubber. After raising your leg, stride toward home plate, then use your back foot to push off the rubber — that will give you added power on the pitch.

PATIENTLY DEVELOP STRENGTH

A big mistake that young pitchers make is to try to throw the ball as hard as they can. That's not the way to pitch. Power pitching comes from strong legs and good mechanics. Use a smooth pitching delivery, focus on the strike zone and the strength in your fastball will come later.

ZERO IN ON THE STRIKE ZONE

Concentrate on mechanics and control when you're pitching in Little League. If you can't throw strikes, you won't have any fun, and you probably won't be a pitcher for very long. Wait until high school to work on throwing curves, otherwise you could hurt yourself.

At 6 feet, 10 inches, Randy Johnson threw hard in part because his incredible stride got him much closer to the plate than most other hurlers. With his long arms and huge step, it sometimes seemed as if "The Big Unit" was throwing the ball a mere 20 feet to the catcher.

GENERATE POWER

But if you look closely at Johnson's delivery, or at that of any other flamethrower, you'll notice that these pitchers, no matter their size, all seem to hold onto the ball until the last possible instant. That's because the longer you hold onto the ball, the more kinetic energy you put behind it. You generate torque and power when you unfurl your delivery. That's why you want to take a powerful stride and wait for the arm to get involved later.

Nolan Ryan used a high leg kick to generate incredible power. He liked to refer to his delivery as "a controlled fall" toward home plate, with his whole front side pointing toward the plate.

The idea is to move your body toward the plate to develop more energy for your arm. If you shift your weight back too far initially, you won't generate that energy, and the power will shift toward your trunk too early. You want the energy to shift to your arm as late as possible in your delivery.

Think of it this way: "You cannot throw the ball until your landing foot hits the ground," Ryan writes in Nolan Ryan's Pitcher's Bible. "The foot hits the ground and then you deliver the pitch. It's as simple as that."

One key is to flex your torso forward; don't be rigid. You want to be flexed forward with your head and trunk over your landing knee — that way you maximize energy from your lower body, which transfers to your trunk and whips your arm around as late as possible. You must transfer energy from your lower body to your trunk. If you don't, the arm comes across slowly, with less velocity on the fastball.

Robin Roberts, who coached the University of South Florida's baseball team after his Hall of Fame career, was fond of saying, "If you're going to hurry, hurry late," a reference to the accelerated arm action at the end of the delivery.

USE YOUR LEGS

Remember: You get velocity from your lower body, not from your arm. If you attempt to get it from your arm, you're eventually going to get hurt. Tennis players suffer from a similar strain, known as "tennis elbow," which results from the elbow's compensating for the lack of power coming from the lower body. When this strain is placed on a pitcher's arm over a long period of time, the result is inevitably an appointment for Tommy John surgery.

A pitcher generating power from his legs is really no different from a batter doing the same, as we'll discuss later, in the chapter "Hitting: Power." The power in your lower body creates the bat/arm speed that drives the ball. You can try to muscle it with your upper body, but that won't create nearly as much power.

It's a good idea to use video to analyze your mechanics. Simple video solutions enable you to compare your delivery frame by frame with the deliveries of other pitchers — even Big Leaguers. Perhaps more importantly, you can watch current video of yourself alongside older footage. Video is a good tool for spotting all sorts of mechanical flaws, but in this instance it's especially valuable for comparing your release point to the release points of other pitchers — Major Leaguers or peers — or to a previous version of yourself.

Another key to adding velocity is keeping your back foot in contact with the mound as long as possible as you move your body sideways. You don't want to swing your lead leg out and around; that creates lateral movement, which slows you down. Instead, drive your front hip right at the target while keeping your lead leg bent.

Young pitchers have a tendency to let the heel of their support foot come up too soon, resulting in an incomplete leg drive; you land too early and want to throw too soon. You might tend to want to throw too early if you think that velocity is all about the arm. Remember that the power comes from your lower body.

STRIDE

As a pitcher, you should have a long stride. Flex your back leg and begin your leg drive while completing it with a stride equal in length to your height. To do so takes loose hips (more on that in the next section).

Tim Lincecum's athleticism helps him to generate incredible power. As he balances on the rubber, his torso faces third base and his left shoulder points toward home plate. With his body stretched like an archer's bow, he unleashes tremendous rotational force. His arm merely comes along for the ride. The result is a hard fastball from a 5-foot-11, 170-pound physique.

"It's about efficiency and getting the most out of my body that I can," Lincecum says.

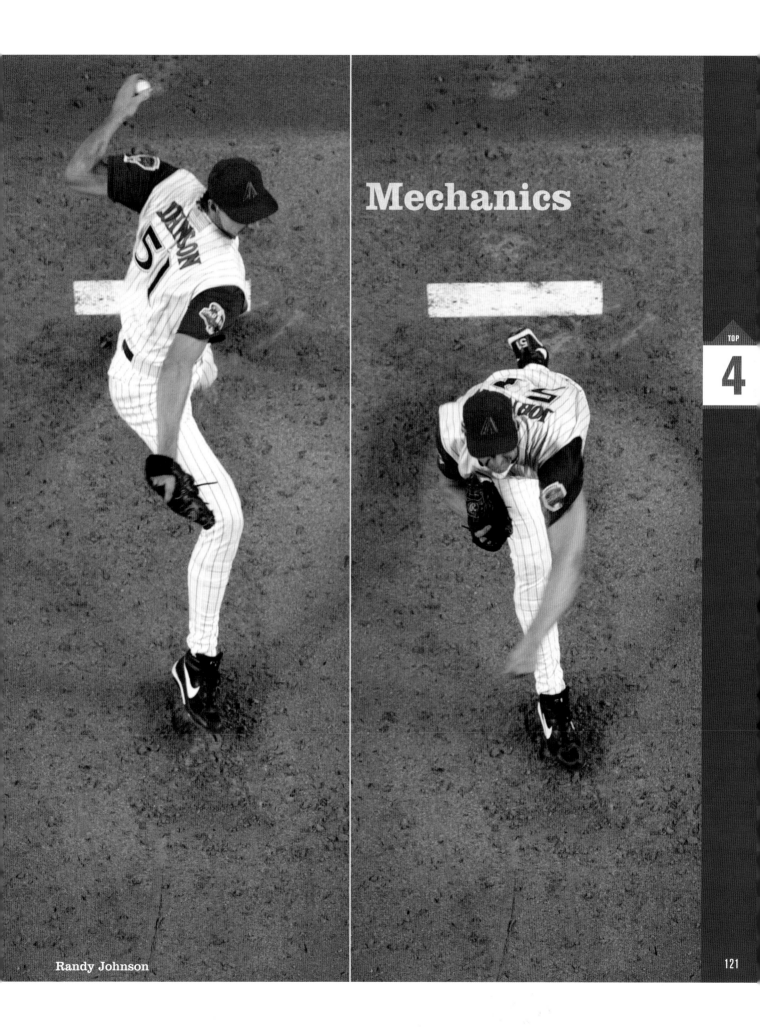

Mechanics

Randy Johnson

VELOCITY
by Joel Zumaya

DON'T OVERTHROW

I don't try to throw as hard as I do — I believe that I was blessed. Rely on your natural abilities and work with what you have. Don't worry about velocity — my velocity came when I was 19 years old. Work on keeping the ball down in the zone. I was an average ballplayer in Little League, not the hardest-throwing guy. I didn't throw hard until I was almost 20, when it all fell into place.

MAINTAIN FOCUS

I get out of whack when I speed up and try to do more than I'm capable of doing — I fly open. Relax, especially with runners on base. Don't speed up. My way of staying focused is to have a really cool attitude. I have one of the quickest deliveries to home plate, so I know that if I get the batters out, base runners can't go anywhere.

KEEP YOUR ARSENAL SIMPLE

I started throwing breaking balls at a young age, but I shouldn't have. Worry about your fastball and change-up when you're developing, and don't forget about your mechanics. Keep your arm up; resist dropping it down. You'll be happy later, when your arm feels strong — as opposed to feeling like it's going to fall off.

Stephen Strasburg

Conditioning

Early in his career at San Diego State, Stephen Strasburg was not considered much of a college prospect, let alone a player who would go on to become the top pick in the 2009 First-Year Player Draft and the most touted prospect in recent years.

But once Strasburg dropped 30 pounds and dedicated himself to a conditioning program, the velocity in his fastball took off. When a pitcher is out of shape, he's not going to have an efficient, powerful delivery that will produce pitches with big-time velocity.

DEVELOP VELOCITY

Even if you're in decent physical condition, you might not be reaching your highest potential velocity if you have not maximized your hip mobility and rotational power. Nolan Ryan and Roger Clemens, two of the game's most durable pitchers, were masters of this; they devoted themselves to training regimens that emphasized the core region, especially the hips and gluteus maximus.

"So much of pitching is leg drive," Clemens says. "Abs also come into play. Keeping those two areas strong is the key to power pitching."

Some pitchers fail to reach their full velocity because they can't execute the proper movement necessary to do so, either because of tight hips or a lack of overall flexibility. The body compensates for weaknesses in these areas by placing more stress on the elbow, knees or back. That stress is a short-term solution, though, and a pitcher will eventually wear down from it.

The idea is to have a loose, fluid delivery, moving as if you are a well-lubricated gate. This is best accomplished through a core conditioning program that emphasizes rotational movements that mimic the pitching motion.

Long before conditioning became the trend in baseball, Hall of Famer Ferguson Jenkins trained by chopping wood, since the motion is similar to the pitching follow-through and strengthens the back and shoulder muscles. These days, pitchers can do a "cable chopping" routine with workout equipment instead of undertaking manual labor. The effect is the same as it was for Jenkins.

ROTATIONAL STRENGTH

Another great exercise for pitchers is a medicine ball throw, described further in the chapter "Conditioning and Drills." Here's how it's done: Stand three feet away from a concrete wall with your shoulders perpendicular to it, holding a medicine ball in front of your waist. Rotate your trunk away from the wall, taking the ball behind your hip. Initiate the throw by attacking your hip toward the wall, following with your trunk and arms, and releasing the ball.

Does this motion sound familiar? The medicine ball, of course, weighs much more than a baseball, but the concept is similar to the pitching motion for building rotational strength.

Catch the ball off the wall with your arms outstretched, and return to the starting position. Try a set of 10 throws on one side, then switch sides. While it's true that you're only going to throw a baseball from one side, you want to have rotational strength throughout your torso and a balanced, flexible physique that can generate power — and velocity — while resisting injury. Training both sides ensures that.

HITTING:

APPRO

Developing an effective batting stance

IT HAS OFTEN BEEN SAID that hitting a baseball is the toughest task in all of sports. To strike a small, round, moving object with a rounded stick is difficult for even the most accomplished baseball players. In no other sport can someone fail 70 percent of the time and still be considered successful.

Parents place plastic bats in the hands of their children and marvel as the tykes swing at anything they can find. Many newcomers to baseball figure such a grip-it-and-rip-it approach works best for beginners; they leave the fundamentals for later.

Anyone who watches Major League Baseball on television sees quickly that there are countless ways to stand in the batter's box. Rickey Henderson crouched low to become as small as possible. Stan Musial also crouched, while Frank Thomas stood so close that he seemed to be on top of the plate. Cal Ripken Jr. was forever tinkering with his stance. And Jeff Bagwell's stance was often described as something that could be best practiced by sitting on a toilet seat.

Bagwell adjusted his approach often early in his career until he heeded the advice of Tony Gwynn, who told him, "When you change your stance so many times, you have no foundation to get back to when you struggle." Musial, who developed his stance to better cover the plate, believed that coaches should think twice before changing a successful hitter's approach, no matter how unorthodox it might be.

Though it might seem like there's no one-size-fits-all method to hitting, many of the mechanics are universal and should be applied to your stance, especially at the youth level.

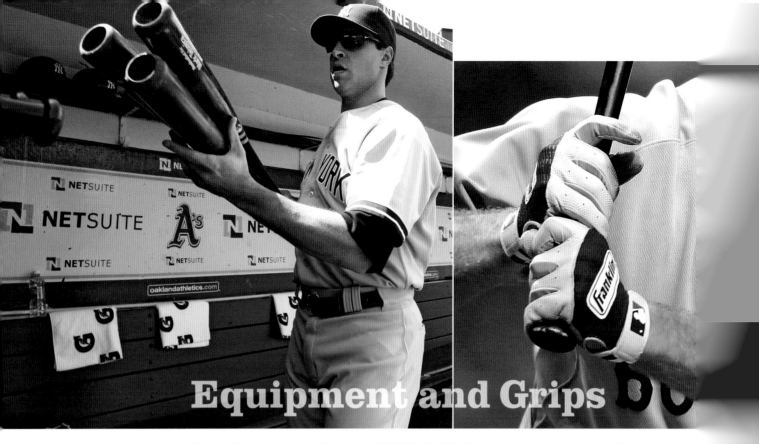

Equipment and Grips

It's tempting for players of all
ages to grab the biggest, heaviest
bat they can manage before
approaching the plate. After all, it
worked for Babe Ruth.

If you're tall and built like the
Babe, Frank Thomas or Dave
Winfield, a larger bat might be
right up your alley. But every
player, even a strong one, should
find the bat that he's most
comfortable with, regardless of its
size. Hitting a baseball is hard
enough without handicapping
yourself further by trying to swing
a bat you cannot manage.

BAT SIZE

A larger bat forces you to use
more of your upper-body power to
swing rather than to use your hips
to drive. But it's harder to
generate bat speed that way and
results in a loss of power. The
ideal swing is short and compact.
Hall of Famer Tony Gwynn, who
won eight National League batting
titles, used a 33-inch, 30 1/2-
ounce bat — one of the smallest in
the Majors at that time. Although
Gwynn was not a power hitter, big
sluggers like Mark McGwire and
Alex Rodriguez have used smaller,
lighter bats, too.

ALUMINUM VS. WOOD

Many non-professional baseball
players swing aluminum bats,
which are stronger and lighter
than wood ones. The added
power of an aluminum bat should
not affect your selection. Go with
the bat that's most comfortable
for you. Parents often make the
mistake of buying their children
larger bats, figuring that they'll
grow into them. But once they
have, the kid has often become so
frustrated with hitting troubles
from an oversized club that he
might not want to play at all.

Players in high school and
college, who are used to hitting
solely with aluminum, should
make it a point to occasionally
practice with a wood bat if they
have professional aspirations — it
makes the transition to the pro
ranks easier.

GET A GRIP

Bat grips are nowhere near as
varied and complicated as golf
grips, but they're not quite
universal either. There are several
schools of thought about how
best to grip a bat. Some believe
that certain fingers or knuckles
should be lined up. But since

everyone's hands are different, it
makes sense that everyone's grip
will vary slightly. To attain the grip
that works best for you, place the
bat at the base of your fingers
and find a grip that's comfortable
in the fingers.

The proper grip allows you to
use your wrists, forearms and
hands to move the bat through
the hitting zone. Baseball is a
game of "loose hands," and a bat
should not be gripped with a
chokehold. Always remember:
Tense muscles slow your swing.

Some coaches tell younger
players to keep their back elbows
up. This position tends to force
the bat deep into your top hand
and can turn a comfortable grip
into an uncomfortable one. It's
better that you focus on being
comfortable than on always
heeding particular guidelines.

If you choose to wear batting
gloves, make sure you go with a
pair that fits snugly and doesn't
wrinkle. When gloves begin to
wrinkle, they cause blisters. That,
of course, defeats much of the
purpose of wearing them in the
first place. Gloves should be so
comfortable that you forget that
you're wearing them.

Stance

Open stance

Closed stance

Like everything else in baseball, you want to have a good athletic position at the plate. Your feet should be shoulder-width, or slightly farther, apart and your weight should be on the balls of your feet. Think of your stance in terms of feeling your butt underneath you. As you're standing and pumping the bat, you will naturally feel your backside under you if you're in a balanced position.

There are countless variations to the baseball stance, but they generally can be grouped into three categories: open, closed and straightaway. Since the

stance is just a starting position – a way for a hitter to get relaxed in the box – it's okay if it is a little out of the ordinary.

An open stance means that your front foot is farther from home plate than your back foot. A closed stance is the opposite. A stance should never be too closed, though, since the batter never wants to affect his vision of the ball, which is tough enough to see as it is. The straightaway stance, as the name suggests, is one in which the feet are parallel to the plate.

You want to stand at a distance so that when you swing

the bat, you cover the entire plate. If you stand too far away and your bat only covers half the plate, you'll be unable to reach pitches on the outside corner. On the other hand, if you stand too close to the plate, the handle is over a chunk of the plate and the barrel of the bat is outside the strike zone; thus, you will often get jammed on inside pitches. Find the happy medium where you can hit a pitch on the outside corner but also handle something inside.

If you have good plate coverage and you're comfortable, you should not worry too much about anything else.

Straightaway stance

Frank Thomas

Jeff Bagwell

THE BATTING STANCE
by Rocco Baldelli

MAKE IT YOUR OWN

First of all, learn good hitting mechanics, and listen to your coaches. Learn as much as you can about hitting at as young an age as possible. The bottom line is to hit as often as possible. Don't try to emulate weird stances. I watched Julio Franco when I was young — he was all twisted up and really wrapped that bat behind his ear. But remember, Big Leaguers are much stronger than you, so you can't always do what they do. Keep your stance comfortable and basic, with your feet shoulder-width apart and your weight balanced on the balls of your feet.

BIGGER ISN'T ALWAYS BETTER

Stay away from big bats. Use one that you can handle comfortably — I use only a 32-ounce stick, and I used a 28-ouncer as late as high school. You need to focus on bat control, and having a bat that you can handle will help.

MAKE CONTACT

Take a short stride and don't jump out at the ball. You won't hit it any harder by lunging. Stay in control and hit line drives. Making contact and hitting the ball hard is the most important thing — homers will come later. No one learns to hit homers first, then becomes a good hitter later; you need to learn to be a good hitter first.

133

No matter what form your stance takes, you need to be able to bring the bat to a position where you can swing it quickly. First you must cock the bat, going back before you can go forward. The motion is like drawing back the bow to shoot an arrow. It's the same concept behind many sports movements, such as swinging a tennis racquet or golf club, throwing a football or shooting a basketball – the idea is to build momentum. It's easier to swing the bat forward if you first put it in motion.

BUILD MOMENTUM

Several things have to happen before you can pull the trigger and swing. First, the pitcher has to wind up and get to his release point. Take your hands back and pick up your front foot so that you can move forward under control as the pitcher does this. Set your front foot down softly in a balanced position – think of stepping on a pillow.

STRIDE

Stride length will vary from player to player. Unless it's so long that it causes your hips to lock, there's nothing to worry about. The hips generate power, and if your hips are tight and locked, you're never going to be able to execute the movements necessary to be a successful hitter at any level. This is not usually a problem for younger players, but, given our sedentary lifestyles, it's important to keep your hips loose by following a core strengthening routine like the one discussed earlier in the book in the chapter "Conditioning and Drills."

"The hips set the swing in motion and lead the way," Ted Williams wrote in his book *The Science of Hitting*. "If they are restricted – if you don't open them wide enough – the wrists will roll prematurely. They won't stay in that strong position long enough to make proper contact."

WEIGHT TRANSFER

The stride starts the weight transfer by taking pressure off your back foot and allowing your hips to rotate. Your body weight shifts forward until your front leg provides resistance. The stability of your front leg gives you the leverage to drive the ball. This pattern of stride, hip rotation, weight transfer and follow-through must be executed seamlessly, though, if you are going to be successful. It might already be a familiar movement pattern to you if you've participated in other sports, because it's the same leverage principle used by golfers, tennis players, boxers, soccer players and athletes in almost every other sport.

Weight Transfer and Stride

LEAD WITH THE KNOB

You might hear coaches talk about taking the knob of the bat to the baseball. They don't mean this literally; you're not going to use the bat as a cue stick. What they intend is for you to lead with the knob of the bat, with the palm of your top hand facing the sky. Your fingers are wrapped around the bat, of course, but, if the bat were not there, your palm would be facing up.

By leading with the knob, the barrel head of the bat stays in the hitting zone. Swing through the zone, follow through and finish high. You don't want to finish across your body. Keep your head down throughout your swing and keep your body balanced. The less movement you have, the better of a hitter you will be.

Don Mattingly, the former Yankees great and AL batting champion who then got into coaching and managing, tells players: "Swing down on the ball as if you're chopping a tree with an ax. But finish the swing – don't stop at the point of contact."

Your follow-through is important. This seems obvious, since the momentum of the bat is coming forward. But many young players make the mistake of connecting with the ball and not finishing their swings strongly.

IMPROVING WEIGHT TRANSFER AND STRIDE

Two great drills used to work on weight transfer and stride are hitting from a tee and soft-tossing. These drills are applicable for all skill levels; even Big Leaguers do them routinely before games.

When you hit from a tee, you don't have to worry about picking up the release point of the ball from the pitcher's hand. You can focus your effort on stance, weight transfer and stride. Set the tee to a height that's comfortable, and work on leading with the knob of your bat and keeping your head down. Maintain balance and think about your hip rotation, weight transfer and stride. Don't be afraid to miss or to strike the tee. If you hit into a net, you don't have to chase the balls. If not, you can enjoy seeing where they land.

It helps if a teammate or coach can feed the balls to the tee for you, but this is one drill you can definitely do alone. There's a reason many youngsters start the game by playing Tee Ball. Hitting from a tee forces you to get in the same position every time and execute the same stride and follow-through. It's still a valuable drill long after you've graduated to the next level.

During soft-toss, you work the same movements as you do when using a tee, but your main goal is to think in terms of having quick wrists and loose hands. Grip the bat loosely, and concentrate on using your hands and wrists to swing. You need a partner who tosses the balls from the side or from behind a net or screen for this drill. You'll be hitting into a net for this one. You also can do this drill with plastic balls.

The tosser should give the hitter good, consistent throws at a fairly quick pace. You shouldn't go so fast that the mechanics of your swing are compromised, but fast enough so that the emphasis is on having loose hands.

HITTING APPROACH
by Tony Gwynn

GIVE IT YOUR ALL

You can make hitting as easy as you want or as difficult as you want. If I was to tell an 8-year-old what to do when going up to the plate, I'd say, "See the ball, hit it and run like heck."

LEARN THE BASICS

One thing about hitting is that the basics are still the basics, whether you're in the Major Leagues or Little League. You have to get your front foot down as the pitch is coming, and bring your hands up in a hitting position. Then you have to be in a balanced position and take a balanced swing. If you do all of those things consistently, you're going to be a good hitter.

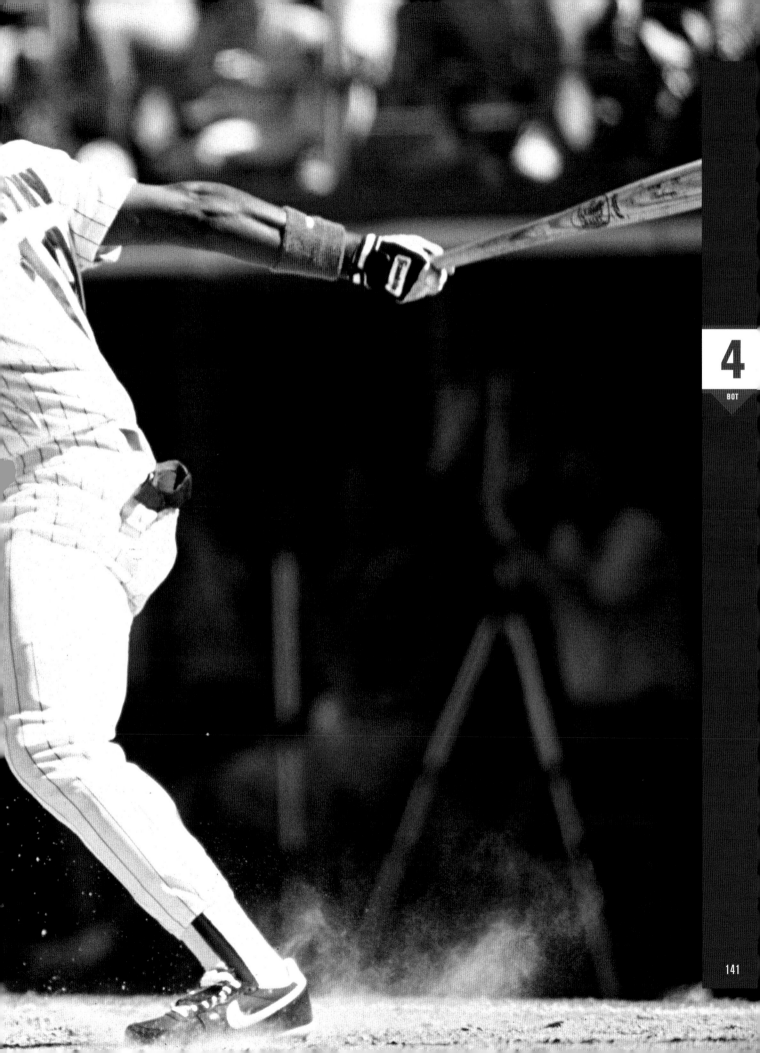

HITTING:
CONTA

Evaluating footwork, arm extension and staying inside the ball

NOW THAT WE'VE DISCUSSED STANCE, weight transfer and stride, we've got hitting mostly covered, right? Not exactly. A batting stance is a work in progress. Some of baseball's greatest hitters have gone through a number of changes in their approaches to hitting during their careers.

While the approaches may fluctuate, the fundamentals remain the same. Ted Williams, widely considered the greatest hitter who ever lived, and Charley Lau, a former Big League hitting coach, influenced many professionals and amateurs with their best-selling books on the topic.

Williams believed that the key to hitting resides in the hips, whereas Lau preached the importance of weight transfer. *Both* play key roles, of course, though Teddy Ballgame never believed in the Lau method of releasing the top hand after making contact with the pitch and, thus, following through with only the lower hand on the bat.

Lau, who served as the hitting coach for five teams, most notably the Kansas City Royals during the 1970s, believed that a one-handed follow-through provided maximum extension of the arms and enabled the bat to maintain a flatter plane through the hitting zone. Walt Hriniak, a disciple of Lau's who served as a hitting coach first for the Boston Red Sox and then for the Chicago White Sox from 1989–95, also taught his mentor's methods. Followers of the Lau/Hriniak method included George Brett, Wade Boggs, Carlton Fisk and Frank Thomas.

Williams' book, *The Science of Hitting*, stresses the importance of keeping your weight back and waiting as long as possible before swinging on each pitch. The swing, he says, should be angled slightly upward so that you can drive the ball in the air. By swinging up, you put the bat on the same plane as the pitch, which is coming from the mound on a downward trajectory.

Lau was more a proponent of hitting to all fields and thought that most hitters lacked Williams' ability to hit slightly up on the ball without dipping their shoulders and popping the ball up. Instead, Lau advocated hitters moving their hands down to the ball, leveling their swing through the hitting zone and finishing upward, in the shape of a "V."

In 1986, Peter Gammons arranged for Williams, Boggs and Don Mattingly to have dinner during Spring Training to discuss hitting and the multitude of approaches to it for a story that appeared in *Sports Illustrated*.

After moderating the discussion for an hour, Gammons concluded that the three agreed that the basics of the Williams and Lau approaches were the same; they were just debating semantics. Four years later, Boggs wrote his own book about hitting — *The Techniques of Modern Hitting* — and concluded that, indeed, *both* Williams and Lau/Hriniak were correct.

Boggs illustrates how you can borrow from several approaches to make yourself a great hitter. The key is to determine what works for you and to recognize that the fundamentals are the same — everything else is just semantics.

Maintaining a balanced position in the batter's box is the foundation of good hitting, and footwork is especially important to that. Think of your feet as providing a rock-solid base from which to hit.

So many young players set up in the box with a good stance, only to fidget and move their feet around as the pitcher gets ready to deliver. Their feet or heels often come off the ground, and soon it's as if the batter is dancing or tiptoeing around the box — so-called "happy feet" are usually a symptom of nerves or anxiety, and it's not a habit that's conducive to becoming a good hitter.

Hitting a baseball is a tough enough task without sending a message to the pitcher that you're intimidated about the at-bat. Not only does fidgeting take you out of the game mentally, but it also makes it physically difficult to hit the ball if your feet are wandering all over the box.

MAINTAIN BALANCE

Wandering feet make it tough to maintain balance and control over your lower body, which are crucial elements to an effective stance. Instead of evenly distributing your weight on the balls of your feet, you're more likely to let your weight shift to your heels or forward onto your toes when you move your feet around the box. You're robbing yourself of power, since this motion takes leverage away from your legs. Furthermore, you lose your sense of timing and, of course, look like someone without a plan at the plate.

AVOID FIDGETING

How do you avoid happy feet? Bending your knees more than you're used to can help, making it harder for your feet to wander.

Remind yourself that your feet are the firm foundation of your stance.

Getting rid of your nerves can be a little more challenging. Step out of the box with your front foot and take a few deep breaths. Channel those nerves into a laser focus on the pitch. The more confident you look, the more confident you'll feel.

BUILD MOMENTUM

A little movement is okay. Just as you don't want to be a statue in the field, you don't want to be rigid at the plate. Move your body in a slow, rhythmical manner, back and forth, until the pitcher begins his wind-up. Not only will this relax you, but it will also keep your hands and wrists loose.

Remember to start your swing with your body in motion, not still. After all, you have to build some momentum to load up your swing and hit the pitch.

Footwork

PICKING UP THE PITCH
by Jeff Bagwell

DON'T OPEN UP

Try to pick up the ball as early as you can. That helps keep your head down, your shoulders square and your hands back behind the ball. Keep your head and shoulders down when you swing. I've gotten hit and hurt by pitches because I was "flying open" on my swing. Opening up exposes everything, so step toward the pitcher when you swing.

COMFORT IS KEY

It's not true that a big bat helps you hit the ball farther. If you feel good swinging your bat, then that's all that matters. The same goes for your batting stance — find something that feels comfortable and stick with it.

BE CONFIDENT

There is no way that you can flinch when a pitcher lets go of the ball and expect to make contact. You need to stay in the zone and rely on your natural reactions at the plate. Most importantly, you must have confidence to hit, so get out there and practice!

147

Coaches are forever telling batters to keep their heads down when they're hitting. The reason for this instruction is that the more your head moves, the more your vision is taken off the plane of the ball, taking your body and bat off track, as well.

Wade Boggs, who won five American League batting titles, referred to this process as "keeping your head quiet."

"When I bat, my head stays locked in a hitting position as if I were hypnotized by the pitch," Boggs wrote in his book, *The Techniques of Modern Hitting.* "My eyes move to pick up the ball, but the plane from which I view the pitch never changes."

Where your head goes, your body will follow. Keep your head still and make it the last part of your body to leave your swing.

Ted Williams was blessed with 20/10 vision, but such sharp eyesight is not necessary to keep a good eye on the ball. George Brett kept his head still on every swing. Pete Rose literally never took his eyes off the ball – he would turn and watch it hit the catcher's mitt, watch the return throw to the pitcher and remain fixated on the mound as the pitcher rubbed up the ball.

Quiet Head

Hands on the Bat

Ted Williams believed in keeping both hands on the bat throughout your swing. It's tough to argue with the greatest hitter of all time, but many of baseball's best players have adopted a swing in which they release their top hand and follow through with only their lower hand on the bat. Some, like George Brett, were Charley Lau disciples, but others, such as Alex Rodriguez, also have taken similar approaches.

THE FOLLOW-THROUGH

Some argue against letting go of the bat because they believe it limits your follow-through, compromising your power on your swing. That might occur if you let go upon or shortly before making contact. Instead, the idea is to let go just after you make contact with the pitch to get maximum power and full extension through the ball as you finish your swing.

Proponents of letting go suggest that the two-handed finish decreases bat speed because the top hand has to stretch for you to complete the swing and thus decelerates your swing to prevent injury. By letting go, they claim, you don't slow things down.

So which approach is the correct one? Go with what comes naturally. If you find yourself letting go and hitting effectively, that's probably the approach for you. Otherwise, keep both hands on the bat.

Albert Pujols

As noted, many Big Leaguers use Charley Lau's methods, but many other people might not be aware of the light-hitting back-up catcher who batted just .255 in parts of 11 Major League seasons yet went on to become a renowned hitting instructor.

Lau created a list of "Ten Absolutes of Hitting," advocating his approach to every at-bat. His list includes a balanced, workable stance; rhythm and movement in the stance; a weight shift from firm backside to firm front side; a stride with the front toe closed; a bat in the launch position – at a 45-degree angle, behind the back ear; an aggressive move toward the pitcher; a tension-free swing; a stance with your head kept down through the swing; use of the entire field; and a swing through the ball (no top-hand rollover, but a top-hand release).

THE TOP HAND AND THE WEIGHT SHIFT

Lau believed in keeping the head down all the way through contact because you can't hit what you can't see. The weight shift from your back leg to your front provides leverage. Releasing your top hand from the bat gives your lead arm the necessary extension

to swing through the ball, maintain bat speed and keep the bat-plane level. Such a level swing, finishing high, creates backspin. That backspin gives your hit loft and distance.

George Brett was struggling as a rookie for the Royals in 1974 when he turned to his hitting coach, Lau. A dead-pull hitter at the time, Brett adjusted his stance, began shifting his weight and started swinging through the ball with good arm extension.

"Releasing the top hand and the weight shift were foreign to me," Brett explained to the New York *Daily News* in 2007. "I think they were foreign to a lot of people. But if you watch Major League Baseball now, Lau has had a tremendous influence on the stars of the game today."

Tony La Russa was the manager of the Chicago White Sox in the early 1980s when Lau was the hitting coach there. La Russa points out that perennial All-Star Albert Pujols' approach is a descendant of the Lau theories. "Isn't it amazing that a majority of the top hitters in baseball let go of their top hand and are weight shifting?" La Russa says. "It happened somewhere, and Charley started it."

The on-deck circle is not just a place for loosening up before a plate appearance. It's also where you can gather information for your approach to the plate.

You should begin mentally preparing for your at-bat while still in the dugout. Study your teammates when they're at the plate and the way that the pitcher approaches them. Imagine yourself at the plate, and picture yourself making solid contact. Such basic sports psychology methods have proven to go a long way toward a hitter's success at the plate. You want positive thoughts to fill your mind before you step into the batter's box to attempt sports' toughest feat.

PRACTICE SWINGS

When you approach the on-deck circle, don't get distracted by family and friends in the stands. Keep your focus entirely on the pitcher, his approach and his various pitches. Loosen up with the bat along with a doughnut or a second bat for added weight on your practice swings. This will make the bat you use at the plate feel lighter – yet another psychological technique that can go a long way. Observe how the ball is moving, and practice swinging along with the pitch, perfecting your timing.

Note the movement of the ball and the sequence of pitches. This is especially important if it's your first at-bat of the game or the first time you've ever faced the pitcher.

As you step into the batter's box, be confident. Don't let doubt enter your head. Don't focus on the pitcher's appearance or expression. You should be concerned only with getting a hit. Be aware of the game situation and whether you're expected to bunt or hit and run. Check to see how the defense is playing. Be selective, but stay confident, too.

On-Deck Focus

STEPPING INTO THE PITCH
by Cal Ripken Jr.

CONTROL YOUR SWING

Step into the pitch and take a level, controlled swing. It's important not to swing too hard and to stay within yourself. I learned to be a good contact hitter before I learned to hit home runs, so don't make a habit of swinging for the fences.

PERSONALIZE YOUR STANCE

There's no set rule for how to stand in the batter's box. The main thing is to work on balance. Learn where you're comfortable and don't be afraid to experiment with your stance — it's a very individual thing.

DON'T CHOKE THE BAT

Pick a bat that feels right to you. There's no general rule about weight, but make sure you can control your bat in a good, short swing. Your grip shouldn't be too tight. In other words, don't choke the bat, but tighten your grip as you begin the swing. Start out by aligning the middle knuckles on your top hand with the middle knuckles of your bottom hand. That will make it easier to turn your hands over and maintain a level swing all the way through so you won't be as likely to pop the ball up.

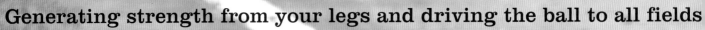

HITTING: POWER

Generating strength from your legs and driving the ball to all fields

EVEN NOW, YEARS AFTER THE Big League home run binge of the 1990s and early 2000s, the longball is still the most exciting moment in baseball.

If, as many have suggested, hitting a baseball is the most difficult task in sports, then launching a home run is perhaps the most impressive accomplishment of all. Not only does a player have to possess a body that's capable of generating enough hip rotation, torque and bat speed to hit such a blast, but he must also combine it with hand-eye coordination and a mastery of mechanics to make the connection.

Is hitting a home run about size or technique? It's obviously about both, though even a skinny player can hit for great power. Ken Griffey Jr., who arrived in the Majors as a rail-thin teenager, became one of baseball's most dangerous longball threats. Yet he never thought of himself as a power hitter, reiterating a familiar refrain that a player cannot go up to the plate thinking home run.

"You go up looking to make good contact and, if you do, the ball will go far," Griffey says.

The great Hank Aaron, a lean 6-foot, 180-pound outfielder, did not possess incredible size and strength like Harmon Killebrew or Frank Robinson, but he might have exhibited *the* best technique by any power hitter in the game's history. Early in his career, Aaron was a terrific line-drive hitter who went with every pitch. Gradually he learned to be more selective, waiting for pitches he could drive.

When eight-time batting champion Tony Gwynn was still playing, he would occasionally talk with the late Ted Williams about the merits of hitting for a high average versus hitting for power. Williams, who did both throughout his career, did not believe the skills were mutually exclusive and told Gwynn that he should be hitting more home runs.

In 1997, Gwynn hit a career-high 17 homers and belted 16 more the following season. Before that, he had shown a tendency to resist inside pitches, one of the reasons he had consistently hit for a high average and rarely struck out.

"Ted said there are situations where you know you'll get something inside and you have to just let it go," Gwynn says. "If you ground out, you ground out. If you fly out, you fly out. But you have the confidence to do it and take whatever comes with it.

No matter how much success you've had in this game, you have to have the confidence in yourself to do something different."

Most players don't need to be talked into pursuing the longball. Some talk about hitting a home run the way golfers describe hitting a perfect shot — they don't even feel the ball.

Jose Canseco believed that his ability to hit for power compensated for insecurities he had playing the game while growing up and helped get him out of slumps.

"It's not just about how far you can drive the ball," he says. "It's a perception, an aura that you carry with you. It's a sense of respect. Your presence alone is power, and you have to earn it over time. You want to project that type of power and authority, because baseball is a humbling game and you won't feel powerful all the time. When you're slumping, you hope you're projecting power to make up for that; otherwise, you have no chance."

There's no need to bulk up to be a power hitter. The game's history is replete with examples of small second basemen who could hit the ball out of the yard, from Rogers Hornsby to Joe Morgan to Dustin Pedroia. Players of any size can improve their power to all fields through training and technique.

Hank Aaron

A LEVEL SWING
by Fred McGriff

SWING AWAY

One of the things that I think kids are scared of is striking out. When you're a kid, you should only be worried about being aggressive and swinging the bat hard. Don't be afraid to strike out. I struck out, and every other Major League batter has struck out, too. It's part of the game.

STAY LEVEL

Another important thing to do is swing down on the ball. If you're trying to hit the ball over the fence, you'll probably pop a lot of balls up and not get a lot of hits. Swing down, concentrate on hitting the ball hard, and power will come later. I wasn't much of a home run hitter in Little League. I learned to be an aggressive hitter as a youngster and didn't start hitting home runs until after high school.

When it comes to hitting for power, which aspect is more important: your upper or lower body? A strong case can be made for either.

HIP ROTATION

Power is generated through the torque you produce through your hips and midsection. Think of your body as a spring uncoiling or as a snake ready to strike. Slugger Kevin Youkilis personifies this, positioning himself with the core of his body spring-loaded, rocking up and down at the plate.

When you can turn your hips and produce ferocious power with your swing, you have the foundation to hit the ball a long distance. Some of the power comes from conditioning. Modern core programs, like the ones discussed earlier, in the chapter "Conditioning and Drills," emphasize hip mobility and flexibility. So-called "hip separation" allows you to wait a split-second longer before bringing your bat through the hitting zone, increasing power.

BAT SPEED

But it's not all about your muscles, either – it's also about your bat speed. Even smaller players with quick wrists can hit for tremendous power. You can have all of the movement in the world with your legs, but if you don't have quick wrists, you're not going to hit for power – or for a high average, for that matter.

Your bottom hand on the bat is important to hitting for power. That's the hand that generates bat speed, which determines how far the ball will go.

"I want to hit the ball as if I'm slapping it with the back of my bottom hand," says longtime first baseman Carlos Delgado. "I want my bottom hand to get to the ball as quickly as possible. And when I finish off my swing, I want to get good extension."

Your top hand gives you that extension. If the top hand comes through the hitting zone too hard, it will roll over your bottom hand. When that happens, you put too much topspin on the ball. Instead of the ball carrying, the swing

produces weak ground balls. You want to produce backspin on the ball, which is accomplished by hitting slightly underneath it. It's difficult to think about this and make it happen, but if your top hand does not come through too hard, it will be natural.

Your bottom hand keeps your top hand from rolling over. If your bottom hand leads the bat through the zone, it's tough to roll over. Leading with the bottom hand gives you more control of the bat, and thus more power.

Kevin Youkilis

Upper and Lower Body

The Power L

The Power L may sound like the name of a boutique bat company, but it is actually a key part of hitting for power. It refers to the rotation of your hips ahead of the hands and shoulders. Your hands rotate with the back shoulder, and the result at the point of contact is an "L," formed from your shoulder to your top hand. The hitter's head is locked on the ball, but should he focus instead on his arms, he'd see a perfect letter "L." Try swinging a bat slowly, and you'll get the idea.

5

BOT

LEG POWER
by Albert Pujols

FIND YOUR BALANCE

Hitting is all about balance, all the time. You want to have a strong base — 60-40. Basically you want to have 60 percent of your weight on your back leg and 40 percent on your front leg. I get my base here, almost by squatting.

DIG IN

Like a fighter in boxing, you need to get your power from your legs. It's the same thing in baseball: Your power comes from your legs. As I finish a swing, the bat head starts to come through the hitting zone. Now my front leg is bent just a little bit, and, very importantly, my back leg is dug in firmly.

STAY INSIDE THE BALL

The idea is to stay "inside the ball," meaning you want to keep your hands — and the barrel of the bat — in, close to your body. You don't want to be reaching out with your arms and extending out, because that will knock you off balance. You don't want to swing with an uppercut, but if you cut down too much, with more of a downward swing, you will only hit ground balls. Stay inside the ball — you get a lot of power doing that. When I'm in the batting cage, I like to use the tee to help keep inside the ball and be consistent. That's the key — being consistent. You develop power from that, too.

Some of baseball's greatest players have been dead-pull hitters. From the great Ted Williams to, more recently, David Ortiz and Carlos Pena, there have been players who rarely hit to the opposite field.

There's nothing wrong with that approach, though at times teams will shift their defense accordingly and make it difficult for you to get a base hit — hitting it out of the park negates such a defense, though.

HITTING TO THE OPPOSITE FIELD

Hitting to the opposite field is often a by-product of swinging too late. But the conscious ability to hit the outside pitch and go the other way is a terrific weapon to have in your arsenal at the plate. If you can take advantage of those defenses that have shifted, you can help your team *and* your batting average.

Early in his career, left-handed hitter Reggie Jackson looked for the inside fastball to pull over the right-field wall, as he famously did many times in postseason play.

As he got older, he learned to go to the opposite field more often, prolonging his career. In contrast, the right-handed Dale Murphy, the great Atlanta Braves slugger of the 1980s, had always tended to go deep to the opposite field more often than he pulled the ball.

There's a tendency to associate hitting to the opposite field with bloop hits and cue shots through the infield. But there's no reason you can't hit the ball the other way for power. For starters, you must have proper plate coverage to reach an outside pitch, which is any ball on the outside third of the plate.

Think in terms of letting the ball get deeper into the hitting zone. Once you recognize that the pitch is going to be on the outside third of the plate, let the ball get deep. Your normal contact point for an inside pitch or a ball in the middle of the plate is over the front edge of home plate. But when hitting the outside pitch, let the ball travel a little farther into the hitting zone. This can be a tough concept to grasp since, after all, the ball is

moving at a high rate of speed. But with a little practice, you'll get the hang of it.

DRIVE THE BALL

You have a natural inclination to swing as soon as you've identified what pitch is being thrown and figured out where it's going to cross the plate. When swinging for power — on a pitch inside or outside — you need to wait an extra fraction of a second longer. You might miss the ball a little more often by doing so, especially at first, but it's a skill that has a huge upside in terms of generating power to all fields.

Power hitters tend to stand deeper in the batter's box. The more time you have to look at the pitch, the more likely you'll be in position to drive it. Place your back foot on the horizontal line in the batter's box closest to the catcher. This positioning will give you more time to recognize the pitch and to time your swing, but make sure that you don't interfere with the catcher.

Your swing is a chain reaction. The heel of your back foot comes

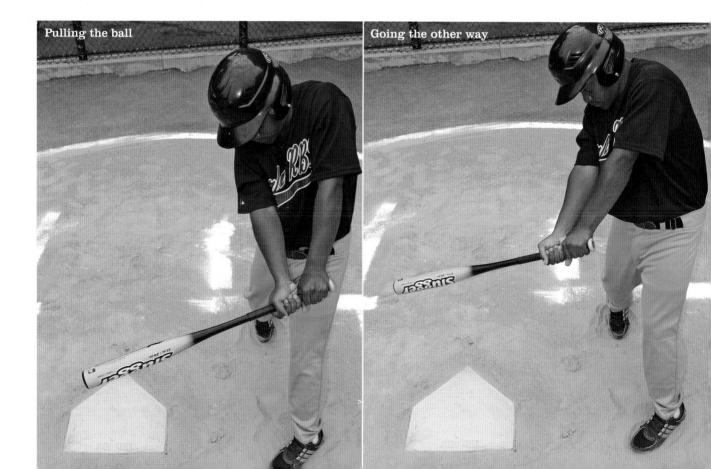

Pulling the ball

Going the other way

Driving the Ball to All Fields

Like Adrian Beltre proves, it's important to retain proper hitting mechanics at the plate, even on an inside pitch: Your rear foot pivots and your hips rotate, while your upper body and bat follow.

up while your foot pivots toward the pitcher. Your hips rotate, and your upper body follows. Your wrists come forward, followed by your hands. Because you're letting the ball go deep into the zone, you're not going to make contact as far out in front.

The angle of your bat will be slightly different than it is when approaching an outside pitch, but you're still looking to hit the ball on the barrel. You're going to execute the same swing as you would on any other pitch, being just as aggressive. Don't think of your approach in terms of slicing or flicking the bat at the pitch. This will, at best, produce the cue-shot, groundball out.

TURNING ON AN INSIDE PITCH

The inside pitch can be the toughest ball to handle, especially if you get jammed. Some hitters tend to let the inside pitch go and wait for a better pitch to hit, but that surrenders a lot of the plate to the pitcher, especially if an umpire has a wide strike zone.

There's no reason not to hit inside effectively – and with power. With the inside pitch, your hips rotate a little more and you make contact with the ball farther

out in front of the plate. Like the outside pitch approach, the idea is to retain your mechanics. You're still going to initiate the swing with your back foot. Your rear foot pivots, your hips rotate and your upper body follows suit. The difference is that your hands follow a path closer to your body than they do for the outside pitch.

The reason that your hips must rotate more on an inside pitch is because the contact point will be farther ahead of the front foot than it is with an outside pitch. You still want to get the bat barrel out in front.

Coaches will often tell hitters to "stay inside the ball," a phrase that refers to the path that your hands should take: inside the path of the pitch and your body. It's a short route to making contact, which is why coaches will also emphasize taking a compact swing at an inside pitch.

A compact swing can generate incredible power. It's important not to think in terms of "turning" on the ball, even though that's what's happening. You don't want to roll your wrists or straighten your lead arm. Instead, you want to keep a slight bend in your front arm. If that arm locks, you lengthen the swing.

COACHING
TIPS

Fostering a winning attitude, handling umpires and utilizing video

COACHING BASEBALL, LIKE PLAYING THE sport, is a rite of passage for many adults. There is no shortage of books written by adults who have learned valuable life lessons from their experiences coaching youth baseball.

Baseball, in theory, is a simple game — you hit the ball, you catch the ball and you throw the ball. At the same time, baseball can get complicated in a hurry with all of the mechanics, strategy and nuances involved. With one-sport specialization and year-round play becoming commonplace among young players, it sometimes seems as if youth baseball has become a pre-professional curriculum rather than just a leisurely game.

The danger, of course, arises when kids no longer find the sport fun. Baseball, with its slower pace, can seem outdated to a generation of kids weaned on video games and the Internet. It's important for coaches to emphasize that it's still the same wonderful game it has always been.

"The great part about kids is that you still see an honest enthusiasm about the sport that we sometimes forget when we look at the Big League game or how serious the game is, even at the Minor League level," says Hall of Famer Cal Ripken Jr., who operates the Ripken Baseball youth program. "It's challenging when there are other sports and activities you're competing with, but the sport is healthy at the grassroots level."

As they are with many endeavors, kids are more likely to be lifelong baseball players, or at least avid fans, if they learn the

sport between the ages of 5 and 8. During those years, they still view almost everything they encounter as new and exciting.

Of course, parents and coaches often hear the familiar "baseball is boring" refrain from kids. The sport does not provide the constant action of hockey and basketball, the physical contact of football and martial arts, or the aerobic workout of swimming and running. Even Big Leaguers struggle to get excited about many Spring Training drills.

At the same time, there are few sports that provide better lessons in teamwork, hand-eye coordination, flexibility, speed and handling adversity than baseball. One of the universal truths of baseball is that even the finest hitters succeed just 30 percent of the time, and even the best pitchers in the game are occasionally told to hit the showers early.

Baseball "is supposed to be hard," says Tom Hanks' character, Jimmy Dugan, in *A League of Their Own*. "If it wasn't hard, everyone would do it. The hard … is what makes it great."

That lesson is a tough sell to kids, who quickly learn that practice and repetition are the foundations of success in baseball. Even the most enthusiastic players can get bored if they perceive practice as work. The key for coaches is to be creative and use teaching methods that excite kids.

Instead of lining players up for a round of fielding fly balls, start a knock-out competition to see who can catch the most. Hold a scrimmage during the last 15 or 30 minutes of practice to foster friendly competition. If possible, spend more time in batting cages than on traditional batting practice on the field, which leaves many players idle. Focus on drills, such as rundown plays and relay throws, that involve a number of players.

Eugene Heyward, the father of Atlanta Braves outfielder Jason Heyward, spent countless hours shuttling his son to practice and games. Asked what advice he would give parents about raising kids in baseball lifestyles, the elder Heyward stressed making sure your child is still enjoying the sport.

"We asked Jason every year, 'Are you still having fun?'" he said. "I asked him when he was a junior in high school, and he looked at me like I was crazy. After that, I stopped asking."

Coaches must remember to be patient and to explain things thoroughly, a lesson that Hall of Famer Rod Carew learned when he opened a hitting clinic near his home in Anaheim, Calif., after retiring in 1985. Many of his students were Tee Ball and Little League players learning to swing a bat for the first time.

"It taught me how to be patient," Carew says. "You can't get upset with kids. You have to tell them what you think will help them and show them how to do it."

Having a winning attitude is not necessarily about wins and losses, though a positive outlook and success often go hand in hand. Many a youth baseball player has endured a stint with a hot-tempered, stern, taskmaster coach, one who takes all of the fun out of the game. Such coaches tend to put undue pressure on their players, too often producing poor results, which contribute to a further escalation in the coach's temper. A downward spiral only continues from there.

When Joe Maddon became the Tampa Bay Rays' manager after the 2005 season, he was struck by the poor attitudes he saw in the team's clubhouse. Was it the result of the team's history of losing since its inception in 1998? Or did the players' attitudes actually contribute to the losing record?

That year Maddon stressed three guiding principles that could work well for coaches at any level. "To me it's all about accountability, consistency and trust," Maddon says. "Those are the factors that permit you to take something negative in a relationship and turn it into something good. I really knew that to get change, you have to change people and the way that people think."

Maddon expected players to be consistent in their efforts, be on time for practice and games, and be accountable for their performance – whether it be team or individual – not blaming others or game conditions for any mistakes. Consistency and accountability foster trust between coaches and players and also among players themselves.

Predictably, Maddon rarely finds himself in a heated altercation with his men, who respect his approach at the helm. Under Maddon's guidance, the Rays transformed from one of baseball's worst teams to one of its best.

A winning attitude manifests itself in many ways. Are you a player or coach who is upbeat every day, encouraging everyone? Do you embrace every role with enthusiasm, even if it's not the one you'd like? Are you willing to put the team's needs ahead of your personal goals? Do you constantly strive to improve and take direction with a positive attitude? Do you hustle on every play, even if the game is out of reach? Do you get along with everyone?

If a player can answer yes to all of those questions, that's all a coach can ask of him – even if he boasts only modest talent.

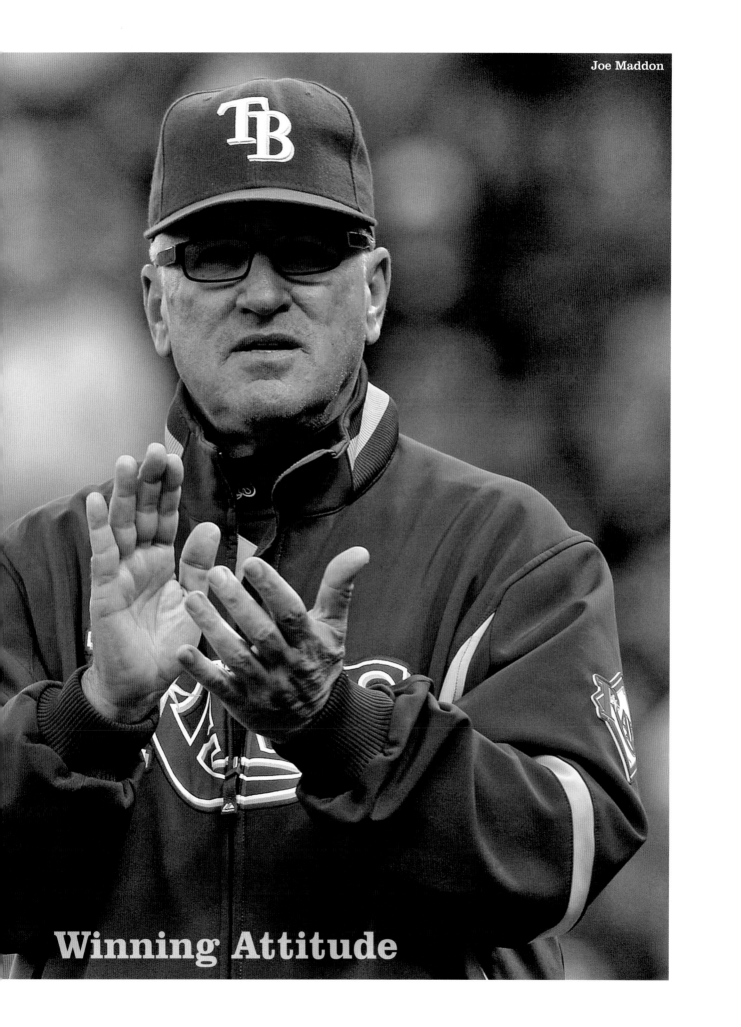

Joe Maddon

Winning Attitude

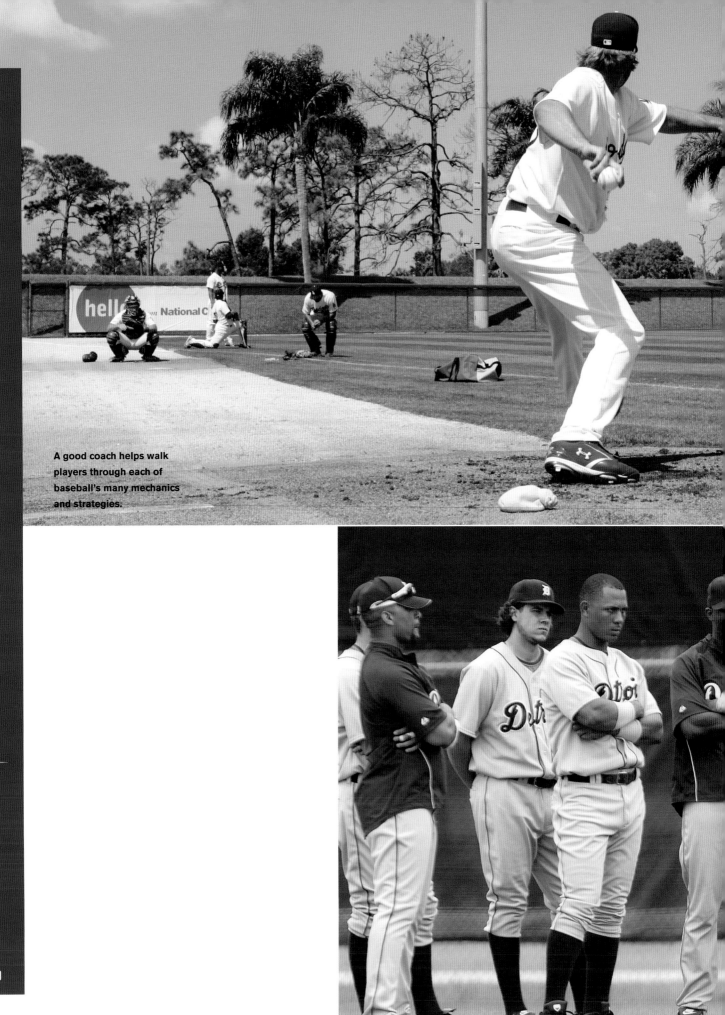

A good coach helps walk players through each of baseball's many mechanics and strategies.

TEAM PLAYER

Eric Hinske is one example of a player who has built a solid career around a winning attitude. The American League Rookie of the Year with the Toronto Blue Jays in 2002, he never became the perennial All-Star that people expected him to be. But rather than bemoan his inability to hold a consistent spot in the lineup, he transformed into a versatile utility player, becoming just the second Major Leaguer ever to play in the World Series in three consecutive seasons for three different teams (2007 Red Sox, 2008 Rays and 2009 Yankees).

"I come in and accept my role, whatever that is – whether it's to pinch-hit or to play a key defensive role," Hinske says. "There's no real secret to it, just do the best you can and try to fit in. It's definitely counterproductive to be a bad clubhouse guy."

It might be a coincidence that Hinske was on each of those teams. Or it could be that teams sought out a player with a proven winning attitude. No matter what your level of play, your attitude will go a long way toward determining your success. Coaches should set the tone for their players.

Eric Hinske

TOP

6

SET AN EXAMPLE

Take Bobby Cox, for instance. Cox won a staggering 14 division titles in 15 years managing the Atlanta Braves from 1991–2005, commanding universal praise from his players for his low-key, simple-rules approach. He never yelled at players or spoke poorly about them, demanding only that they show up on time and play hard.

Coaches could learn from that approach, as well as from Cox's uncanny ability to pick players up after they had contributed to a loss.

"You'd come off the field with your head down, having just booted a ball or something," says two-time National League MVP Dale Murphy, the great Braves outfielder of the 1980s who applied Cox's teachings while coaching several of his sons' teams, "and there's Bobby saying, 'Man, that ball took a wicked hop, didn't it?' You're thinking you should have made the play, and you should have. But, the point is, sometimes it's just a matter of how the ball bounces."

Umpires make mistakes.

Players, coaches and fans have a natural tendency to want to take their anger out on umpires for those mistakes. At the Big League level, managers make a great show of arguing with umpires, both to support their players and perhaps to swing the next close call in their favor.

At the youth, high school and college levels, criticism of umpires by players should never be tolerated. A coach's attitude toward umpires sets the tone for how his players will act. Coaches should have a no-tolerance policy when it comes to their players criticizing umpires and should heed that policy themselves as often as possible.

If your league does not have a policy toward parental behavior already, insist that parents of your team refrain from making comments about the umpiring.

One way to teach players respect for umpires is to give them a first-hand look at the job.

During an intrasquad scrimmage, have players don extra catcher's gear and play the role of home plate umpire, or give them batting helmets and assign them to work the bases. Encourage high school and youth players to umpire the games of younger kids. If you're a coach, volunteer to work some games yourself. You'll come away with a new appreciation for the job – and how well the umpires do it, even at the youth level. Think about it: In what other profession is it your goal to do your job exceptionally well and take no credit? Only when there's a controversy does anyone pay attention to the men in blue.

"The best an umpire can hope for is to walk off the field unnoticed," says Randy Marsh, who umpired in the Majors for 29 years before retiring after the 2009 season.

KEEP IT CIVILIZED

If, as a coach, you have a disagreement with an umpire, focus your discussion on the rule or game situation in question. Many arguments can be diffused with a simple clarification of the rules, which the umpire no doubt knows better than you do.

"You can have what appears to be a very heated argument when really it's just a discussion of the rules," says longtime Big League umpire Dana DeMuth.

If, after adopting a calm, appreciative approach to umpires, you still have an argument, do not let the situation fester. No matter what level of baseball you're coaching, there's a good chance that the same small group of umpires calls your games on a regular basis. Apologize for your behavior, even if a video replay proves that you were right and the umpire was wrong.

"When an incident has occurred, I've sought the umpire out to smooth over hard feelings," says longtime Big League manager Tony La Russa. "I cannot afford to have that linger."

Umpires

Video

Early in his career, Hall of Famer Tony Gwynn would cart two video recorders with him on the road — one for taping the game on clubhouse televisions and the other for editing footage afterward in his hotel room.

In 1983, not long after his wife, Alicia, gave birth to their son, future Big Leaguer Tony Jr., the couple purchased video equipment to document his early days. But they soon found a more professional use for it when the elder Gwynn fell into a dreadful slump: Gwynn had Alicia tape his at-bats. When he saw the tape, he immediately recognized the problem, corrected it and rolled through the rest of the season, finishing with a .309 average.

These days, as head coach at San Diego State, Gwynn can quickly pull up video of any of his players on a laptop computer. Such footage is invaluable for pitchers, hitters and, of course, coaches. They can see, like Gwynn did, if a player has developed a mechanical flaw or bad habit. They also can track progress over time or use it to review an upcoming pitcher that the team has previously faced.

Because of the technological advancements of the last three decades, it's also possible for a Little League parent to shoot games and edit video for immediate review. Given the accessibility of technology, youth teams have the same tools as pros at their disposal. If a parent or sibling of one of your players is taping the game, ask if he or she could cut some player-specific footage or make multiple copies of the entire game to review.

As for video games, their sole value is entertainment. Some young players, perhaps trying to justify time spent with controller in hand, will stress the realism of baseball video games and how playing them can improve their real-life mastery of the game.

That's not necessarily the case, says Gwynn Sr., an avid video game player who refused to play baseball-related games during the season.

"Some of these games are so realistic, I'd go out on the field and be all out of whack because I had made adjustments to the video pitcher," he says. "And sometimes he'd be better than the real guy."

ADVANCED
FUNDAM

Executing bunts, relays, double plays and the hit-and-run

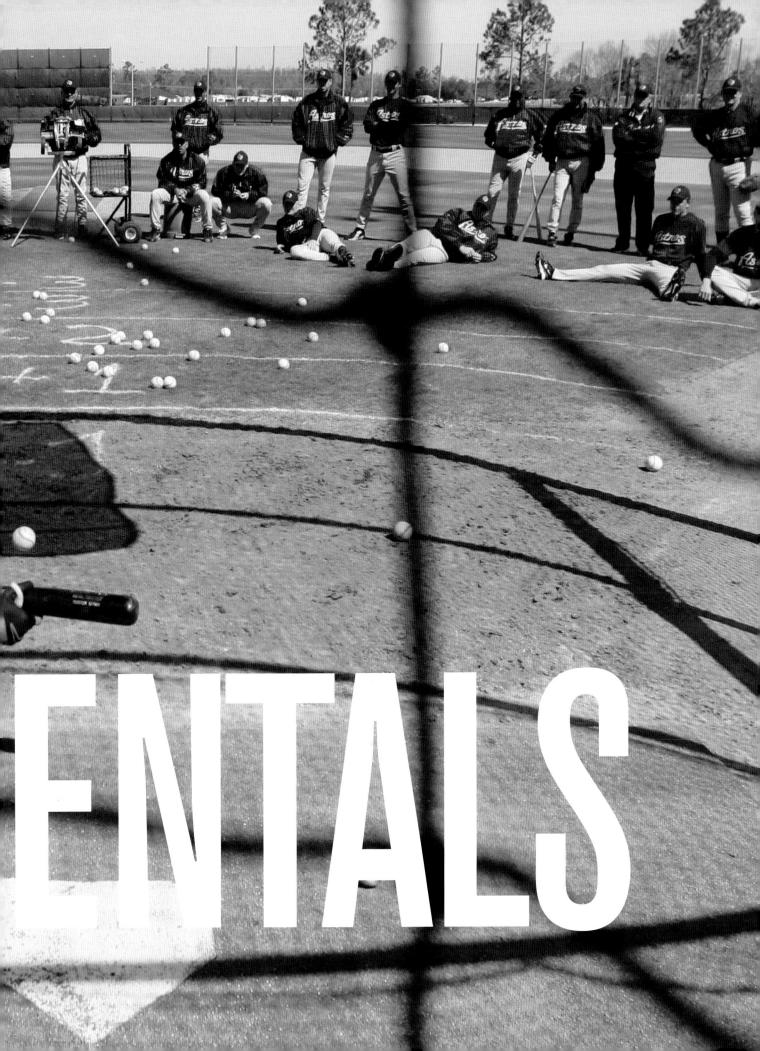

ENTALS

UNLIKE MANY TEAM SPORTS, BASEBALL does not consist of many diagrammed plays that require a nod or a shout from the coach. Aside from the hit-and-run, the suicide squeeze and the pitchout, most baseball "plays" are nothing more than the execution of advanced fundamentals that occur routinely depending on the game situation.

But that doesn't make them any easier. In fact, such plays can be even *more* complicated than anything that a football or basketball coach can draw up on a chalkboard. These advanced fundamentals are carefully choreographed offensive and defensive maneuvers requiring lots of practice and execution, usually by more than one player at a time.

Square-around

Some people believe that the only bunting that belongs in baseball is the red, white and blue fabric draped around ballparks for special events.

In recent years, several statistical studies have suggested that it's not worth sacrificing an out to move a runner along. Drag bunting can produce base hits, but many players would rather work on conventional hitting than on one of the less glamorous parts of the game.

Whether you like it or not, bunting, either for base hits or to move runners forward, plays a key role in baseball. When your team needs to advance a runner into scoring position, especially late in the game, the batter needs to know how to lay down a sacrifice bunt. When the defense is playing back, or you're facing a pitcher who is not giving up hits, knowing how to drag bunt comes in handy.

"Guys with speed should utilize it more," says veteran outfielder Juan Pierre, one of baseball's best bunters and fastest players. "The bunt puts pressure on the defense. The threat of it alone puts pressure on the defense."

Knowing how to bunt makes you a more versatile player. Coaches will be less likely to pinch-hit for you in a bunt situation if you can execute the play. Plus, you can boost your batting average with a few well-timed bunt hits.

"I wouldn't have been in the Bigs for 17 years if I couldn't bunt," says former outfielder Brett Butler, who holds the record for bunt hits in a season with 41 for the Dodgers in 1992. "Bunting is not giving in to the pitcher. It's adding to your talent to make you a more complete player."

THE SACRIFICE BUNT

The traditional method for a sacrifice bunt is the "square-around" approach, in which you open your stance completely with your entire body perpendicular to the plate and facing the pitcher. The problem with this position is that it commits you to a bunt. To swing away or drag bunt, you have to step back into a normal hitting stance before attempting either, and you likely won't have time to make the adjustment. Plus, the square-around position leaves you vulnerable to getting hit by the pitch.

Bunting

Pivot-in-place

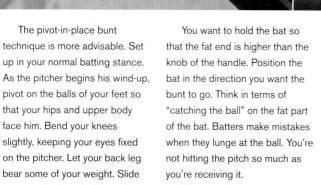

When attempting a bunt, it's important for your top hand to grip just below the barrel of the bat. Make sure to keep your fingers behind the bat to protect them.

The pivot-in-place bunt technique is more advisable. Set up in your normal batting stance. As the pitcher begins his wind-up, pivot on the balls of your feet so that your hips and upper body face him. Bend your knees slightly, keeping your eyes fixed on the pitcher. Let your back leg bear some of your weight. Slide your top hand up the bat and re-grip the bat firmly just below the label by using your thumb and the top side of your index finger. Your other hand should stay in place on the handle by the knob of the bat. The key to this technique is to hold the bat away from your body, just above the belt, tucking your fingers behind and just below the barrel — you don't want the ball hitting them.

You want to hold the bat so that the fat end is higher than the knob of the handle. Position the bat in the direction you want the bunt to go. Think in terms of "catching the ball" on the fat part of the bat. Batters make mistakes when they lunge at the ball. You're not hitting the pitch so much as you're receiving it.

"Use your legs," says former Big League second baseman Roberto Alomar, a skilled bunter. "Think of it as playing catch. You know how you bend your knees when you're making a catch and then straighten them after you've made the grab? It's just like that when you bunt."

Just because you're bunting does not mean you should commit to a ball that's not a strike, though. To take the pitch, bring the bat back across the strike zone and return it to your shoulder, reverting back to a normal stance in the process.

If you're looking to sacrifice, it's okay to show the bunt early. When you're looking to bunt for a base hit, though, the element of surprise is a factor. In this case, wait as long as you can before showing bunt.

THE SQUEEZE BUNT

With a suicide squeeze, it's okay to bunt the ball right back to the pitcher, since your teammate is running from third. Here, too, it's important to wait as long as possible before showing bunt. Wait until the pitcher releases the ball before you begin to pivot.

6

BOT

NETSUITE

BUNTING by Mark Grudzielanek

DON'T GIVE IT AWAY

Bunting for a hit is an important way to help your team win. Do it right, and it's a beautiful thing. If you move your back foot forward too soon, it gives the third baseman an extra second to react. Wait until the pitcher starts his motion, then drop your hands and push the barrel of the bat out in front of you.

CATCH THE BALL WITH THE BAT

The barrel should be above, or resting on your hands. Grip the bat firmly, with your top hand no farther up the bat than the label. Keep your fingers and thumb under and behind the bat, with your thumb pointed up, then hit the top of the ball and bunt it down.

GET THE BUNT DOWN

You can't run before you bunt, so keep the bat out in front, where you can see it and watch the ball right onto it. What I like to do is point the head of my bat toward first. That way, when the ball hits the bat, it will roll down the third-base line.

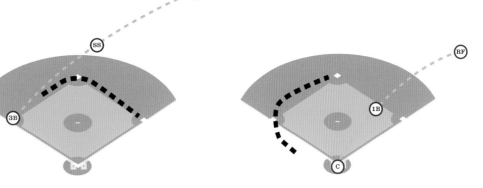

Relays and cutoffs often are used as interchangeable terms in baseball, but they are not necessarily the same thing. A cutoff man, as the term suggests, cuts off a thrown ball and redirects it elsewhere – to catch an aggressive trailing runner, for instance, especially if there's little hope of nabbing the lead runner.

In the Big Leagues, where most outfielders have rocket arms, an infielder is more likely to play the role of cutoff than relay man, even though the positioning is similar for both jobs. At the youth level, where outfield arms are still developing, the cutoff man assumes the role of relaying the ball to the appropriate base.

KNOW YOUR CUTOFF MAN

The game situation often determines where the ball is thrown on a relay. For outfielders, the key is to make good throws and to hit the cutoff man, who is your relay partner. If you're the left fielder throwing to third, the cutoff man is the shortstop. If you're throwing home, the cutoff man is

the third baseman. If you're the right fielder throwing to third, the cutoff man is the shortstop. If you're throwing home, the first baseman is the cutoff man.

Kids need relays to reach second base, too, sometimes. When the right fielder throws to second, the second baseman acts as a cutoff while the shortstop covers the base. The shortstop is the cutoff man on a throw to second from left and center fields.

As the cutoff man, you must position yourself to manage the throw. You should know, from practice, the arm strength of the outfielder making the throw and position yourself accordingly in the outfield.

RECEIVE A CUTOFF THROW

As an infielder, you should line up between the base and the outfielder and make yourself a big target. Your hands should be above your head and you should be in an athletic stance that will enable you to move in any direction to field a bad throw.

Listen for directions from the infielder at the base behind you to determine if you need to cut off the throw or allow the ball to go through. Get a good read on the flight of the ball when it leaves the outfielder's hand. After angling your body in the direction of the base you're throwing to, catch the ball chest high on your glove side. You might have to move forward to catch a weak throw, but, whatever you do, keep the ball off the ground if possible.

One of the oldest axioms in baseball is never to overthrow the cutoff man. That only holds true part of the time. If an outfielder has a strong arm, he should try to throw to the base *through* the cutoff man, either on the fly or on one hop. In that situation, he has only overthrown his relay man and the ball has gone where it should. But if it's a situation where the cutoff man will dictate where the ball should be thrown next, it's important that the outfielder not overthrow him so he can catch the ball easily and quickly decide where to throw next.

Hit-and-Run

The hit-and-run is one of the most beautiful plays in baseball when it's executed properly. It frustrates the defense by generating a hit from what might otherwise have been an out (or two). The purpose of the hit-and-run is to open holes in the infield defense, avoid the double play and advance a runner from first base to third. The hitter's job is to protect the runner. When the play is called, the batter must swing at any pitch in order to keep the catcher back, even if the ball is in the dirt or at eye level. Ideally, the ball is hit on the ground toward the second baseman's typical fielding position. But because he's covering second for the steal, the ball shoots through the infield and everyone is safe. Hitters can practice this play by hitting down on the ball.

The runner breaks for second as he would during a stolen-base attempt. Great speed and a good jump are not as important, but the key is to make the play look like a steal attempt to force the middle infielders to cover second base. That opens up more ground for the ball to get through the infield.

ON THE PITCH

As a runner, make sure that the pitcher has committed to throwing to the plate. Once you're sure that's where he's heading, break for second. After a few strides, look at the hitter and pick up the ball. If the hitter swings and misses, you're now in a steal attempt situation.

Bunting and the hit-and-run are not the only special situations a batter must consider. With a runner on second base and nobody out, it's your job as a hitter to advance the runner to third. Bunting toward third base is one option. Driving the ball to the right side is another. The idea is to be aggressive with your swing while looking for a pitch that you can hit on the ground to the right side of the infield.

OTHER HITTING SITUATIONS

With a runner on third and less than two outs, the infield will sometimes be playing in. As a batter, you want to get a pitch you can drive. A sacrifice fly is a good outcome of an at-bat in that situation. If the infield is playing back because the team has a big lead and is willing to give up a run in return for an out, a ground ball is also a good outcome.

If you're the runner at third when the infield is playing in, take an aggressive lead, as far away from the base as the third baseman is. If you're instructed to go on contact, sprint toward home when the batter connects with the ball. Chances are that you'll be safe because the infielder will opt not to go home with his throw or that the ball will get through the infield. But you might also be out at the plate. That's okay, though; it's the coach who takes the risk with the call, and it will take perfect execution on the part of the defense to nail you at the plate.

A double steal can also be a good option. The key here is the runner on third, who must time his break to the moment when the catcher commits to throwing to second base. If the catcher's throw is to the pitcher or to a middle infielder who relays the ball back home, the runner will likely be out at home, but that's the risk a team takes for such aggressive play.

Double Plays

Double plays may look smooth and easy, but they're actually the result of well-executed moves, usually by three players.

Double plays begin with the way infielders position themselves with a runner on first and fewer than two outs. The second baseman and shortstop will "cheat," shifting two steps in and two steps toward second base from their usual positions. This shift is so that they can get to the bag in time to handle a throw.

The second baseman takes a direct route to the base to field the ball from the shortstop or third baseman. Begin behind the bag with your left foot on the base. As the ball comes in, square your shoulders as you come across the bag to receive the ball. As you come off the base, shift your weight to your right foot and throw to first. Be sure to open your left toe toward first base, which better stabilizes your front leg and helps protect against serious knee injuries.

For a ball hit to the right side of the infield, the shortstop is the middleman. Put your right foot on the base with your shoulders squared to the player who is throwing the ball. As the ball is thrown, move across the bag and make the catch. Be sure to close off your left shoulder before you throw so that you can put something on the throw to first.

The main job of the first baseman is to provide a big target, usually not a problem given the typical size of the athlete assigned to the position. He must also dig balls out of the dirt and stretch toward second base to receive the throw as early as possible.

DOUBLE-PLAY SITUATIONS

On a 3-6-3 double play, in which the first baseman fields the ball, the key is for him to make a good

TURNING THE DOUBLE PLAY
by Barry Larkin

PIVOT

Making the pivot on the double play is basically a three-step movement. It's sort of like a dance step. As a shortstop, when you get closer to the bag to accept the throw from your partner, plant your left foot to the side of the bag. Then, as you're receiving the ball, kick the bag with your right foot, then leap out of the sliding runner's way and land with both feet.

MAKE AN ACCURATE THROW

Many coaches preach that the throw should be made to your partner's glove side. I think it's important to throw the ball to his chest every time. And you should always keep your body low, sort of in a crouch, so you don't waste time straightening up to throw.

GET AN OUT

The rule I learned is that if the shortstop's momentum is going toward second base, then you toss the ball to the second baseman underhand. If you're fielding a ball in the shortstop hole and you're a good distance away from the bag, then you have to throw it overhand. Try not to think about all the things you have to do after catching the ball, or you'll make an error. Because the most important thing about turning two is making sure you get one!

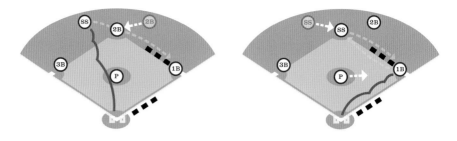

throw to second base. Since this play is more unusual than the traditional 4-6-3 or the 6-4-3, there's a tendency for the first baseman to make an errant throw. It's not because the first baseman has lesser skills than his middle-infield counterparts, but rather that he underestimates how much time he has to make the throw. Take a moment to pivot and make a good throw to second. Make sure that you avoid the runner with your throw, and, even more importantly, make sure that you get that first out at second base.

Usually the first baseman has enough time to get back to the bag to receive the throw from the shortstop. But the pitcher should always hustle over to the base and be ready to make the catch if the first baseman can't, completing a 3-6-1 double play.

When the pitcher fields a comebacker to the mound, the shortstop should cover second to set up the 1-6-3 double play.

6
BOT

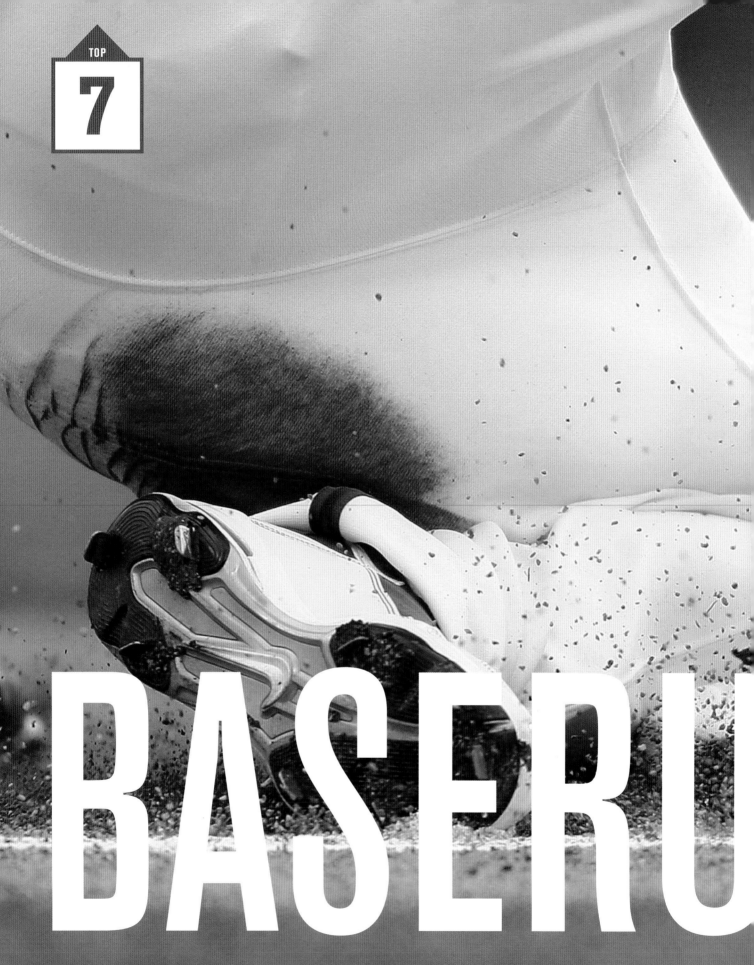

BASERU

Running through the bag, taking a lead, turning corners and sliding

NNING

THERE'S PERHAPS NO MORE UNDERRATED aspect of baseball than baserunning. Since it takes so much effort to get on base, it's important to maximize your opportunities to score runs. Although stealing is a part of baserunning — perhaps its most exciting aspect — it is only one component. Even players without great speed can become elite baserunners by understanding situations, hustling, heeding fundamentals, reacting quickly and listening to base coaches.

Not surprisingly, some great base stealers, like Ichiro Suzuki, Roberto Alomar and Paul Molitor, are also thought of as great baserunners. But some of the best baserunners have been players not known as elite base-stealing threats — players like Derek Jeter, Larry Walker, Cal Ripken Jr. and even Albert Pujols. The difference between being safe or out is often just a fraction of a second — the result of a lead or a quick reaction.

Don Zimmer, who has watched perhaps more baseball than *anyone* in his six-plus decades in the game, gives credit to a Hall of Famer he managed with the Red Sox in the 1970s. Carlton Fisk was a catcher, a 6-foot-3 burly man nicknamed "Pudge," but he was a disruptive force on the base paths, even though he never stole more than 17 bags in any season.

"He always went first base to third," Zimmer says. "He scored from second base on a single. He knew how to get a lead." Just like hitting, throwing and fielding, baserunning involves certain fundamentals. Coaches at first base and third base play a key role in baserunning, but ultimately it's more important for players to rely on their own eyes and judgment.

On Deck

Be an educated player. There's plenty you can do to prepare before getting on base: Take note of how the defense is positioned; watch the other team take infield practice and see which players have strong arms and which do not; pay attention to the throwing arms of the opposing team's

outfielders, both their strength and side. For instance, if a left-handed left fielder has to go to the line to field a base hit, he can't make a quick throw to second very easily. The same is true of a right-handed right fielder ranging to the line.

As the on-deck batter, you are responsible for assisting your

teammates coming to the plate and trying to score. Let the runner coming from third base know if he needs to slide for a play at the plate or if he can come in standing. Tell a batter if the third strike has gotten away from the catcher. And, as a batter, be aware of that possibility yourself.

It's important to take note of where the ball is hit, but don't dwell on your handiwork with the bat. Start running – hard. If it's a ground ball, sprint on a straight line to first base. Hitting a routine ground ball is understandably disappointing. Channel that frustration into digging even harder for the bag. Assume that the infielder will bobble the ball. And keep your head straight; turning to see where the ball has gone will slow you down.

Strike the front of the bag since that's the closest part to you, but not at the expense of running through the bag. Avoid stutter stepping or jumping to the base. Instead, run through the bag another 20 feet, turning to your right into foul territory. Do not slide into first base; Big Leaguers may do it on rare occasions, but it does not get you there any faster, and it can cause injury.

On Contact

On a Base Hit

Once the ball gets through the infield, you should think double. Every runner has his own spot to begin the turn around first base, varying from about halfway to first to slightly closer to the bag. Make an arc in foul territory and round first by touching the center of the edge facing second base with either foot. This creates a "starter's block" effect, similar to a starting block in track, allowing you to push off the base to get an extra burst of speed. Some runners have a tendency to strike the corner of the bag as they make the turn, but the small target increases the probability of missing the bag, slipping or turning an ankle.

Spot the ball again when rounding first base and listen for help from the first base coach. When advancing to second on a potential triple, take the same approach of rounding the base.

After returning to first base following a single, glance to see where the defense is playing. Pick up the pitcher and the base coach. It takes just a second, but it can mean an extra base on a hit by the next batter.

A note on safety: There's a reason that runners keep their helmets on while on base. Live balls are dangerous. Always be aware of the ball, whether it's being thrown by an opponent or hit by a teammate.

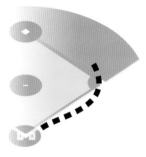

Taking a Lead

Baseball is a game of inches, and a proper lead can make the difference in a game. At the very least, an aggressive lead distracts the pitcher and upsets his rhythm. It also gives you a better chance of taking an extra bag on a hit.

Keep your eye on the pitcher; do not chat with the first baseman or umpire. Hall of Fame Manager Whitey Herzog would tell his players to get a lead of at least 10 feet off first. Of course, his St. Louis Cardinals teams of the late 1980s featured some of the best baserunners in history. Most suggest a primary lead of about eight feet, which translates into three or four steps.

Move laterally, or shuffle, toward second base. Don't cross your left foot over your right foot, because you could end up twisted and easily get picked off. On a pick-off throw, dive or jump back to first instead of sliding, as you lose momentum that way.

AT FIRST BASE
As the pitch is delivered, take a secondary lead of two or three more lateral steps. Be aggressive. While on first, look for signs from the third base coach. Keep track of other runners on base and the number of outs. Take a mental inventory of the arm strength of the outfielders. Be alert and get back to first after the pitch, or the catcher can pick you off.

On a fly ball with less than two outs, move halfway toward second, a good spot to advance from should the ball drop. If it's caught, hustle back to first. On a hit to right field, glance at the third base coach when going from first to third. He can be your eyes and decide whether to send you home. But if the ball is hit to the left, take a look and decide on your own. Still, it's almost never a good idea to run through a third base coach's stop sign.

As a runner on first base, you have important roles on potential double plays: Avoid letting the second baseman tag you; force a throw to second to give your teammate more time to reach first. You also have an obligation to break up double plays by hustling to second and making a strong slide to disrupt the defense, even if you're out by a mile.

AT SECOND BASE
On second, runners can be more aggressive with their leads, since

214

middle infielders are less diligent about holding them on. Take the biggest lead possible without risking a pickoff. Unless you're attempting to steal, the lead can be taken back from the baseline to give you a better angle to round third on a hit.

There's no reason for a player of any speed not to score from second on a hit to the outfield – unless it's a line drive hit on one hop directly to an outfielder.

Focus on the pitcher – he has the ball – and resist looking at the middle infielders. You should be able to see the second baseman from the corner of your eye. Let the third base coach worry about the shortstop.

For grounders hit when you're on second and nobody's on first, the rule of thumb is that if it's hit

to your left, advance to third; if it's hit to your right, wait for it to go through the infield before moving on. If it's hit right at you, make sure the ball doesn't hit you – you'll be called out if it does – and quickly decide based on the location of the nearest fielder.

AT THIRD BASE

On third, the lead is often referred to as a "timed walk" or "walking lead." Take a few steps down the line in foul territory as the ball crosses the plate. Your right foot should strike the ground as the ball enters the hitting zone. Keep your head facing the pitcher but tilted slightly toward home. This gives you the flexibility of moving in either direction – toward home if the ball gets past the catcher or back to third if necessary.

Take your lead in foul territory and head back to third in fair territory after a pitch that doesn't get put into play. If a batted ball strikes you in fair territory, you're out. By going back to the bag in fair territory, you disrupt the catcher's chance to make a play; he either has to throw around or directly at you. If the throw strikes you, it could careen away.

Don't ease up when running home, even if the defense has no shot at throwing you out. Even if it's a hit, if another runner makes the third out before you score, the run doesn't count.

Runners should always be in a position from which they can easily tag up on fly balls to the outfield, especially on foul balls when fielders are in poor position to make plays.

It's not enough to take just an eight- to 10-foot lead. When the pitch is thrown, you want to gain some more ground with what is known as the "secondary lead." This could be as simple as taking a step or two and watching the ball to the plate. But great baserunners take an aggressive approach on every pitch, even when they're not stealing.

When taking off for the next base, you should pivot on the right foot and step with the left. This, combined with staying low, gives you balance and momentum as you sprint toward the bag.

STEAL CLUES

Most bases are stolen on the pitcher, not the catcher. With a right-handed pitcher, the front (left) shoulder gives the runner clues. To throw to first, the pitcher must open his shoulder. To throw home, he must close his shoulder.

Left-handed pitchers present a challenge, as they face first from the stretch. Some give away their pick-off moves by raising their hands higher or opening the right leg when throwing to first.

You can do reconnaissance work before the game, in the dugout or in the on-deck circle. Study the starting pitcher's pick-off move and time of delivery to the plate. Even Big Leaguers adjust. More than six years into his career, Carl Crawford extended his secondary lead a half-step against many pitchers.

THE HIT-AND-RUN

On a hit-and-run play, the jump toward second is the same as it is with a steal attempt. Although the lead need not be as large, it still must look like a steal attempt — the idea is to move the middle infielders toward second and increase the chances for a ball to be hit through the hole on either the left or right side. Because of the more conservative lead, you should never be picked off during a hit-and-run play.

RUNDOWNS

You will eventually get caught in a rundown, usually as a result of overly aggressive baserunning. When there are other runners on base, remain hung up as long as possible to allow them to advance. Force the defense to make many throws. If the defense slips, not only will you be safe, but you will also have advanced.

On the Go

Sliding

Sliding is a key part of baserunning. It's a lot of fun, both in games and in practice, but often is not rehearsed enough. As a result, some young players are reluctant to slide because they fear injury. Such hesitancy, along with a lack of experience, can contribute to injuries.

The basic slide is the straight bent-leg or "figure-four" slide. At full speed, drop down, landing with one leg folded under the other in a figure four. Slide on the side of your calf and hamstring.

Throw your hands up to shoulder level, and do not put a hand down to brace yourself to prevent injury.

Many coaches suggest learning to slide with the left leg extended, though some players do the opposite. That way, when players advance to the pop-up slide, they're in better position to proceed to the next base. Make the decision to slide early and slide hard. Some of baseball's worst injuries occur when a runner hesitates. Slide straight to the part of the bag to which

you've committed – contorting your body to avoid tags can lead to injury. Never slide headfirst into home plate. When in doubt about reaching a base safely by standing, slide. There's nothing more embarrassing than being tagged out when you would have been safe by sliding.

The best way to practice sliding is on grass without shoes. Even when it's too rainy to play a game, it's possible to work on sliding – and sliding on tarps can be loads of fun.

SLIDING
by Chone Figgins

DON'T BE AFRAID TO GET DOWN

It's almost like you are sitting on one leg and extending your other leg. Make sure you fully extend your leg on a steal. Really concentrate on sliding toward the middle or back of the bag — the part away from the plate. That will help you avoid the player trying to sweep the tag on you. The infielder has to come back to tag you, so you want to slide middle to back.

GO FEET FIRST

The feet-first slide is effective for many reasons, especially since it protects your body. But most importantly, if you slide feet first, you can do a pop-up slide, so you can quickly get up and run to the next base if the fielder misses the ball. As your right foot hits the bag when you slide, brace it against the base, and your body will lift itself up. But be careful. You have to make sure not to step off the base, or you can be tagged out.

GET AN EARLY START

An important part of baserunning is knowing when to start your slide. You should know where the ball is and decide if you need to slide soon after you start down the base path. You want to start your slide a full step or two from the base. It's always better to start early rather than late.

TOP

7

219

BASERUNNING
by Eric Young Sr.

MAKE IT QUICK

Anyone, regardless of how fast he is, can learn to be a better runner. You start by developing a knack for running each ball out as if it's going to be a close play. Your first couple of steps out of the batter's box or off a base are the key. I tried to reach maximum speed as quickly as I could. It puts pressure on the defenders, who might make a bad throw. It's also important to keep those first steps short and quick.

PICK UP YOUR COACH

Practice watching your base coaches as you run, too. They're there to let you know whether to hold up, keep going, stand or slide. I looked at the coach when I was about two-thirds of the way to the next base. If the coach signals for you to slide, go feet first. You hear all the time about guys getting spiked or hurt going head first. Go in feet first and hard to let the fielder know you're coming. That way your backside takes the punishment of hitting the ground. If your coach is waving you on, shift into another gear. I call it, "turning on the turbos." When you're rounding a base, use the bag to your advantage. Always go for the inside corner of the bag, and push off as you go by.

BE SMART ON THE BASES

In the end, good baserunning is more than just being able to run fast. It all comes down to knowing your own ability and developing your own instincts. Those are the things that make a great base runner.

Tagging Up

Tagging from third base is one of those golden opportunities to score without the benefit of a base hit – and a perfect example of playing so-called "small ball." On a fly ball deep into the outfield, tagging up is fairly standard procedure. Wait for the outfielder to make the catch and then sprint toward home plate.

On more shallow balls, it's a judgment call. Let the third base coach guide your decision. If the ball is caught by an infielder with his back to the infield, it's generally a good bet to tag up and run home, since the fielder must take the time to turn around and make the throw.

The decision to tag from second base is a much more difficult one. You're already in scoring position and don't want to become a victim at third base. And if the ball caught is the second out, then you won't have the chance to score on a subsequent sacrifice fly anyway.

Still, it's always advantageous to advance if there's minimal risk involved. Having said that, the decision can be a little tricky. If it looks like a routine fly ball, stay on the bag. Wait for the catch and then tag. If it looks like a ball that might fall in for a base hit, it's best to go halfway and then take off once it falls. If the ball is caught, you'll have plenty of time to get back to the bag; you might even have time to get back to the bag and tag up anyway.

FIELDING: CATCH

Handling pitchers, blocking balls in the dirt and framing

AS THE CATCHER, YOU ARE arguably the most important player on the field. You're responsible for calling games and directing pitchers. Because your job is so physically demanding, you must be tough and durable. In many ways, you're the manager *on* the field, which explains why so many former Big League catchers take on managerial roles after retiring from the game.

Contrary to popular portrayals, the catcher is anything but the big kid placed behind the plate because he lacks the agility to play another position. Often the catcher is one of the team's better defensive athletes, since the job requires quick feet, good flexibility, a strong arm and endurance. Carlton Fisk and Ivan Rodriguez may share the nickname "Pudge," but it's simply a reflection of their durable, burly physiques rather than a comment on their lack of athleticism. Then there's Craig Biggio and Dale Murphy — players who began their Big League careers behind home plate and are testament to the versatility of

catchers. Both former backstops transitioned to new roles and went on to win multiple Gold Glove Awards at other positions later on in their careers.

There are few players who make more valuable contributions to a team than catchers who can swing the bat well *and* play the position at an elite level for years — a small fraternity that includes Fisk, Rodriguez, Johnny Bench, Yogi Berra, Gary Carter, Bob Boone, Lance Parrish, Thurman Munson and, more recently, Joe Mauer.

Catching also requires a certain disposition. Not only must you deal with a variety of egos and personalities on the mound, but you also must assume a diplomatic role, mediating disputed calls with the home plate umpire. You must know which pitchers to chew out and which hurlers require a calmer approach from their batterymate. You have a perspective on the entire field and, although you're the leader, you must sacrifice your ego for the good of the pitcher and the team.

"As a catcher, you take responsibility for every pitch," says Berra, the Hall of Famer and New York Yankees great. "You have to know early on what's working for a pitcher. It's not always so easy, because pitchers think they're so smart. You have to handle each one differently. You have to know which guys you holler at, which guys you just pet."

Kevin Costner and Geena Davis famously portrayed the roles of the team leader and catcher in the movies *Bull Durham* and *A League of Their Own*, respectively. In real life, Darren "Dutch" Daulton took charge of the hardscrabble band of journeymen that made up the 1993 Philadelphia Phillies, who won the National League pennant. After developing bad knees from years of wear and tear behind the plate, Daulton was forced to transition to first base. He later joined the Florida Marlins and, in 1997, propelled them to their first World Series title by providing the same kick-in-the-pants leadership that had inspired the pennant-winning Phillies.

"A guy like Daulton can transform an entire team with his personality," says Cliff Floyd, who was a young outfielder with that '97 Marlins club.

Even Bench — the leader of Cincinnati's "Big Red Machine" who is regarded by many as the greatest all-around catcher in history and led his club to four NL pennants and two world championships during the 1970s — points to the leadership role as a catcher's most important duty.

"Catchers have to be in control — of their pitchers, of the game and of themselves," Bench once said. "I could hit and throw as well as any catcher who ever played baseball. But there was more to my job than that. I had to be in charge. When I was behind the plate, there was never a doubt about who was running things on the field."

Because of the inherent danger that comes with the territory, a catcher uses more equipment than any other player – he dons a mask, chest protector, shin guards and protective cup. Different sources credit early Big League catchers Muddy Ruel and Bill Dickey with first referring to catcher's gear as "the tools of ignorance." In either instance, the reference was considered ironic, contrasting the smarts needed to handle the role with the foolishness required to play a position dangerous enough to require so much protective gear.

For obvious reasons, the athletic supporter and cup rank as the most important pieces of gear. Catchers also need to wear a helmet that covers the ears and has a mask strapped to it. The mask should include a large throat protector, too. Hockey-style mask helmets, pioneered by journeyman Big League catcher Charlie O'Brien in the 1990s, also are a good option.

The chest protector should cover not just your chest, but also your groin area and throat with its flaps. Shin guards should cover your kneecaps fully, even in the squat position, and also cover as much of your toes as possible.

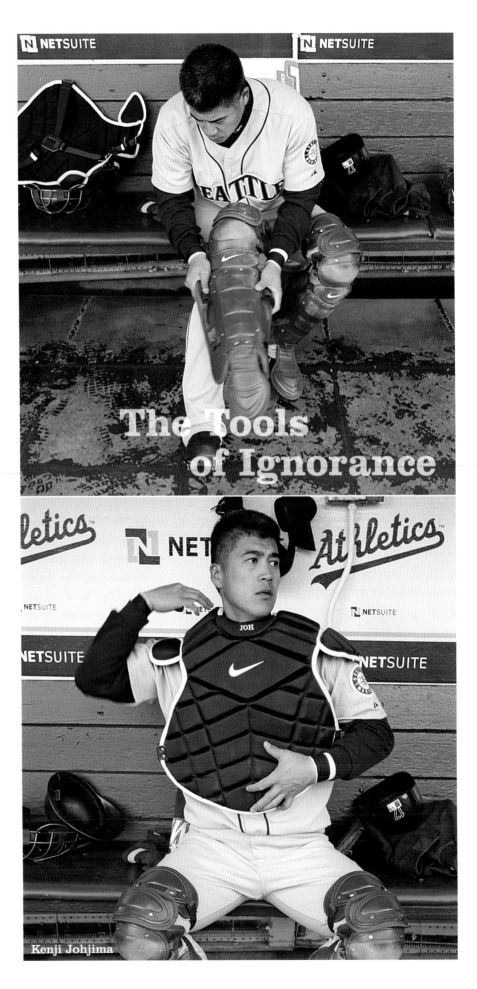

The Tools of Ignorance

Kenji Johjima

RECEIVING
by Ivan Rodriguez

RECEIVE THE PITCH

Use your catcher's mitt to create a good target for your pitcher. If you want the ball on the outside corner of the plate, for instance, put the target there. And when the pitcher releases the ball, watch the ball from the moment it leaves his hand until it hits your glove. When you're in the squatting position, be up on your toes so that you can react quickly if a runner attempts to steal a base or if the pitch is a little bit wild.

I've seen a lot of young catchers receive the ball too close to their bodies. You should catch it out in front of your knees without getting your glove too close to the batter's swinging zone, which could lead to catcher's interference and a free pass for the batter.

USE YOUR TOOLS

Catchers are called "backstops" for good reason. When a pitch is wild or bounces in the dirt, the catcher's job is to block the ball so runners can't advance. A lot of young catchers instinctively turn away from the ball or close their eyes. Remember that your mask, chest protector and shin guards are between you and the ball.

DON'T LET ANYTHING PAST

When a pitch is headed for the dirt, square your body, drop to your knees, keep the ball in front of you and don't turn your head away. If your body flinches on a ball in the dirt, you might block the pitch, but the ball will bounce to the side and runners will advance. Also, try not to open your legs too wide or the ball could skip right through them.

7

BOT

As a catcher, you must provide a big target that the pitcher can see easily. Your glove hand should extend in front of your knees and should not be wedged between them. Your throwing hand should be out of the way to protect it from foul tips. Some younger players like to place their throwing hands behind their backs, but, for others, this hinders balance and leverage. It's better to place it behind the mitt or along the outside of your leg, where it's protected yet in a strong position.

You should give your target early enough for the pitcher to focus on it, but not so early that the opposing team's base coaches or players in the dugout can have time to relay a location sign to the batter. When positioned properly, your back should be straight but not stiff. Your thighs should be parallel to the ground and your weight should be slightly forward on the balls of your feet. Catching feels uncomfortable when you first start to play the position, but soon the

discomfort subsides, your quadricep muscles stop burning and the stance feels natural.

Think of your catcher's mitt as the bottom of a funnel that represents the strike zone. Catch the pitch near your body, but not too close. Funnel the high pitch lower, the low pitch higher and the pitches on the fringes of the strike zone closer to the center. How effectively – and discretely – a catcher frames a borderline pitch often determines if it's ruled a ball or a strike.

Receiving and Framing

Giving Signs

When putting down signs, it's important to keep them simple enough for your pitcher but difficult for your opponents to see. Hold your glove hand in a position that's low on your left to prevent the third-base coach from seeing your signs. Your right knee should keep the first-base coach from seeing them. If there is a man on second, you'll want to go through a series of signs to mask the pitch you're calling. Again, keep things simple. Don't go through more than three, and designate the middle or last sign as the real one. Crossed-up signs can result in wild pitches and passed balls.

7

BOT

Like pitchers, catchers are judged largely by the strength and accuracy of their arms. A catcher with a respected cannon can negate aggressive baserunning. The accuracy of his arm is dictated largely by his footwork.

STEAL ATTEMPTS

With a runner on base, assume that he's stealing on every pitch and be alert. Of course, you still need to focus on the primary task at hand, receiving the ball and framing it for a strike. Catch the ball so that it's easy to retrieve from the mitt and transfer to your throwing hand.

Balance yourself and build momentum by pointing your non-throwing shoulder to the base you're aiming for. When a runner attempts to steal, receive the ball and throw with a controlled step toward the target. It's important that you stay low and not block the umpire's vision, which could cost the pitcher a potential strike.

Steal attempts of third base are less common and are usually the fault of the pitcher for allowing the runner to lead too far off second. The biggest challenge is dealing with a right-handed batter and deciding whether to throw in front of or behind him to make the play at third. On an inside pitch, some batters, like Derek Jeter, lean their upper bodies in, making it easier to throw behind them.

PITCHOUT

The pitchout is a similar procedure. Once the pitcher starts to the plate, the catcher should step into the unoccupied batter's box. Don't step out too early – that's a balk, and the runners will get to advance one base. Ideally, the ball from the pitcher should come in letter-high, but you should be on the lookout for errant throws, as well.

PICK-OFF PLAY

The pick-off play to first from behind the plate is one of the game's more exciting moves and can be initiated by the catcher, manager or first baseman. Calling a pitchout to get a guy who you think is going to steal is the ideal situation, but, if the count is not favorable, a ball on the outside part of the plate will work if the batter is right-handed. When attempting to pick off a runner on first who is taking a big lead, step in the direction of first base to make a throw and remember not to pop up too early and block the umpire's view of the pitch.

Throwing to Bases

Blocking Balls in the Dirt

Not every pitch is going to hit your mitt. Blocking balls in the dirt is a difficult assignment that often can be painful. But there are several steps you can take to keep the ball from scooting away.

Much like a hockey goalie trying to prevent pucks from getting by, your goal as a catcher is to stop an errant pitch from darting to the backstop while keeping it out in front of the plate. For balls that land in front of you, drop to both knees facing the ball. Tuck your chin in to prevent the ball from hitting your neck, and position your throwing hand safely behind your mitt. Your glove should be placed between your legs to protect your groin and to keep the ball from getting through. Lean forward so that your body hovers over the ball, and don't be afraid to use your chest protector to softly deflect it back in front of you. Doing so will prevent the ball from rolling too far upon impact and will make it less likely that runners advance.

The stance is similar with balls to the sides. For a ball to your right, you should drive off your left leg. When the ball is to your left side, drive off your right leg at a 45-degree angle. The goal is to keep the ball out in front and in fair play, making it less tempting for the runners to advance.

Ultimately, you should block wild pitches in any way possible, whether by diving, lunging or even, as a last resort, using a backhand stab. Blocking is especially important with a runner on third base.

Unfortunately, there's no shortcut to practicing how to block balls in the dirt other than having a coach, teammate or machine throw them at you – think of fictitious Cleveland Indians catcher Jake Taylor in the movie *Major League* being pelted for long stretches to hone the skill. The payoff is becoming proficient at blocking errant pitches and saving runs.

BLOCKING PITCHES IN THE DIRT
by Gregg Zaun

SACRIFICE YOURSELF

You have to want to be a catcher. You'll get a little bit more banged up than you would at other positions, but you have to accept it. Be tough. Your most important ability is to really be able to catch the ball. All the other skills become more important when you're older.

MAKE THE CATCH

Your glove should be broken in. If it's properly broken in, it should almost close itself. Keep your palm between the ball and the backstop, and you will be okay. Don't worry too much about it. Use your hands to catch the ball inside of your glove. Use a tennis ball or racquetball to practice. Have someone throw it to you, or bounce it off a wall.

BLOCK THE BALL

When catching, protect your bare hand. Go forward to block the ball. Kick out, and put your knees where your feet were. Going forward, you're more likely to use your chest protector than your shoulder, mask or arm. Make sure you watch the ball all the way into your chest, just like when you watch it into your glove.

7
BOT

233

When it comes to fielding bunts, the catcher might have the toughest job on the field. After all, dealing with balls hit on the ground is not a main part of a catcher's job description. Any catcher who can handle bunts quickly and efficiently is a tremendous asset.

When the ball is bunted in front of the plate, the catcher is in the best position to field it and make a strong throw, since he does not have his back to the bases like the pitcher and charging infielders.

The catcher should call for the ball loudly and scoop it up with both hands – unless it has come to a complete stop – to make it less likely that the ball will be bobbled. With a ball hit down the line, it's often the catcher's decision to field it or wait to see if it goes foul. One way to prepare for this situation is to simulate bunts before the game. The contour and grooming of infields varies by ballpark, and it's important to have a lay of the land on which to base your decisions.

Once you field the bunt, it's important to shift so that your body weight and momentum are going toward the bag that you're throwing to. It's a common mistake to field a ball headed up the third base line, whirl around and throw to first in one motion. This can result in a ball bypassing first base and landing in right field. Be sure to first position your body in the direction of the bag before throwing.

If the ball is bunted beyond your reach, play the role of traffic cop by calling for the player who should field the bunt and where the throw should go.

A botched bunt can result in a pop-up within your reach. If you are prepared and act quickly, you can hustle and snare the ball in the air before it lands.

Defending the Bunt

Unmasked

Wear a mask during all game action, as well as when you're warming up a pitcher. One of the few exceptions to wearing a mask is when fielding a pop-up. As you move in the direction of the ball, fling the mask in the opposite direction of where the ball is likely to land. This gives you two free hands to make the catch and eliminates the possibility of tripping over the mask en route.

Anyone who suggests that baseball is not a contact sport has never witnessed a collision at home plate. Such plays – though exciting to watch – are potentially dangerous for catchers, even with the protection of their equipment.

When a runner attempts to score from third base on a ground ball to the infield or a fly ball to the outfield, or from any base on a ball hit cleanly through the infield, there is the potential for a play at the plate to occur.

BRACE YOURSELF

As the catcher, you should get in a balanced athletic position with your knees bent and positioned shoulder-width apart. Some catchers will get rid of the mask at this point, though it's advisable to keep it on in the event of a collision. Block the plate while still giving the runner a portion of it to slide toward. Your left foot should be planted about 18 inches in front of the plate with your toes pointed toward third.

As you receive the ball, turn your head to see which direction the runner is taking. Don't turn your head too quickly, otherwise you'll risk mishandling the throw.

MAKE THE TAG

Because your left foot is pointed up the baseline, the runner has room to slide to the back of the plate. After receiving the throw, place the ball in your throwing hand inside the mitt. This will prevent the runner from knocking the ball out of your glove. Once the ball is secure, you should push your body down and across the base path, thus turning the runner away.

If the runner opts not to slide and instead attempts to run you over, it's important to maintain an athletic stance, similar to that of a linebacker or a defensive back in football, to brace yourself. The inside of your knee is especially vulnerable, so be sure your shin guards are pointed toward the runner for added protection.

Jason Jaramillo demonstrates
how to effectively block home
plate when a runner is
attempting to score. The ball
is securely in his glove as he
prepares to make the tag.

Guarding the Plate

7

BOT

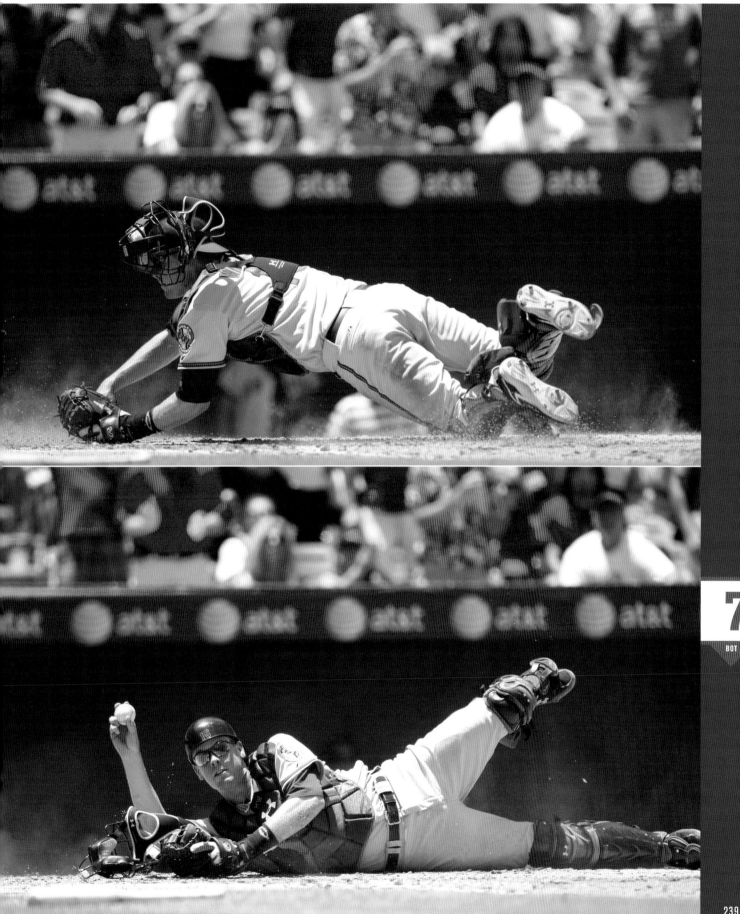

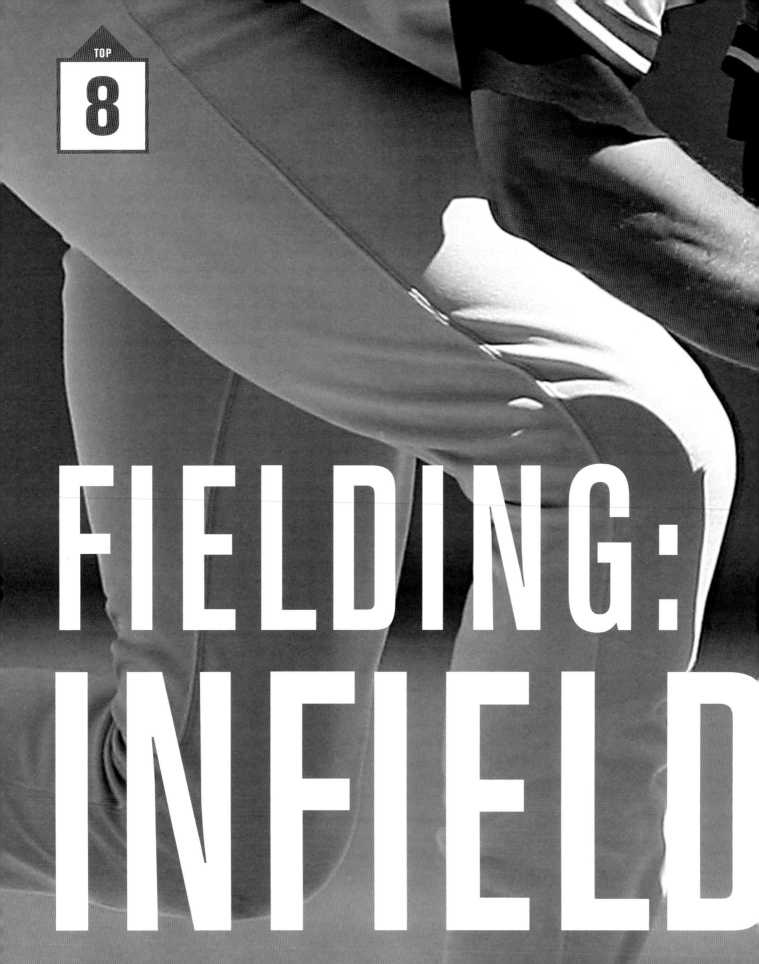

FIELDING: INFIELD

Positioning yourself for ground balls, pop-ups and other plays

OFFENSE, ESPECIALLY THE HOME RUN, is often more exciting than what happens in the field. But good defense can be a game-changer in baseball. Ask any Big League manager what wins games, and chances are that he'll point to pitching and defense, especially in the infield.

Defense, of course, does not reflect in box scores unless a player commits an error. Ozzie Smith, the Hall of Fame shortstop, was maligned early in his career for being *only* a defensive wizard and elite base stealer. Bill Mazeroski, considered by many the greatest fielding second baseman ever, had to wait nearly three decades after his retirement to be enshrined in Cooperstown, eventually being elected by the Veterans Committee.

Sports highlight shows — with their many defensive highlight packages — may be most responsible for boosting the value of defense over the last two decades. In recent years, Major League teams have re-evaluated defense, spending increased amounts of time analyzing the ground that an outfielder covers and the plays that an infielder makes relative to his counterparts at the position. In 2008, the Tampa Bay Rays were transformed from a team that had never experienced a winning season into the American League champions, in part by upgrading their defensive capabilities. Other teams have followed suit, placing a premium on fielding.

"People don't look at defense and consider that it can change the momentum of a game," says Smith, who won 13 consecutive Gold Gloves with the San Diego Padres and St. Louis Cardinals. "But it can do that just as much as an offensive play."

The infield is the first line of defense, receiving some of the hardest-hit balls. Reaction time is key at third base, especially. Each of the four infield positions has a unique job description, though there are common denominators among them in terms of how a player is positioned. Much like a basketball team switching off assignments on the defensive end of the court, a baseball infield operates as a single unit, reacting and moving together.

"Defense is a rhythm, team thing, and everyone's hustling and trying to outdo one another," says former General Manager Pat Gillick, architect of World Series championship teams in Toronto and Philadelphia. "It's great to watch."

FIELDING GROUND BALLS
by Roberto Alomar

GET READY

Keep your knees bent. It's very important to get your butt down and keep it down — the upper half of your legs should be parallel to the ground. Keep your head down the entire time so that you can keep your eyes on the ball all the way into your glove.

RECEIVE THE BALL

As the ball gets close, extend your arms almost straight out and field it in front of your body. Never get caught catching the ball near your body or underneath you. That's called "letting the ball play you," and it leads to errors.

FIELD IT CLEANLY

The most important first step in fielding is to see the ball. Once the ball is hit, get your feet moving toward it and keep your eyes on it at all times. You'll need to follow that ball all the way into your glove if you want to catch it.

TOP

8

Positioning

The so-called "ready" position is similar to that used in other sports: It's an athletic stance, with your knees bent, shoulders square to home plate and weight evenly distributed on the balls of your feet. It's a relaxed stance, but one that allows you the flexibility to scoop up a grounder, break to either side or leap to grab a line drive.

KNOW THE SITUATION

As an infielder, you should be mentally ready before each pitch, knowing the number of outs and the game situation (number of runners on base, possible bunt situation, potential steal attempt, etc.). If applicable, you should know who is covering on a steal or on a hit-and-run attempt. Always assume the ball is coming to you, and know what to do if it does. As the ball approaches home plate, inch forward by taking one or two quick steps or hops. Instead of being flat-footed, you're already in motion, ready to make the play.

For balls hit directly at you, the key is to create a wide base. Anyone who has played infield at any level has heard these words of wisdom: Get your butt down. By doing this, your weight will shift forward and your hands will naturally move out in front. From this position, you can see the glove and the ball at the same time and make the play cleanly. Don't let the back of your glove touch the ground — only your fingertips should go that far, giving you a better chance of fielding the ball.

TO THE SIDE

For a ball hit to your left, your first step should be with your right leg, instead of the one closest to the ball. This crossover step is repeated with your left leg on a ball hit to your right. A crossover step involves simply crossing one foot over the other to initiate movement. This is the best way to move laterally on the diamond.

Balls hit to your non-glove side require a backhand grab, which is more difficult than a forehand play. The idea is still to catch the ball out in front of your body. Field with your left foot down and plant your right foot while closing off your hips and shoulders.

You can also use the sliding technique, in which you range to one side and slide to make the pick-up. The play is made mostly by shortstops, since they tend to cover the most ground of any of the four infield positions. Ozzie Smith and Omar Vizquel, two of the best defensive shortstops ever, could slide on either leg, but that's not always the case.

"Most people learn to slide one way, and that's the only way they can do it," says Nomar Garciaparra, who played much of his career at shortstop for the Boston Red Sox. "I slide on my right knee. I can't slide on my left knee."

MOBILITY

The physical demands of infield defense require a player to move in three dimensions, so it's important to have good flexibility and mobility.

Flexibility helped Roberto Alomar, one of the best second basemen ever, bounce back up after sliding to grab a ground ball. "It helped me slide-step a runner trying to knock me down at second base to break up a double play," Alomar says. "My ability to run, slide, lunge and bounce back up helped me win 10 Gold Gloves."

HANDIWORK

While footwork is important in defense, many infielders are revered for having "soft hands" in the field — meaning they absorb balls rather than let the balls bounce off their hands.

Evan Longoria, the Gold Glove third baseman for the Tampa Bay Rays, spends time during infield practice working on this technique by fielding balls from his knees before each game.

"The idea is to use my hands," he says. "You can't move your feet in that position. Normally, you use your feet to field the ground ball. You don't use your hands as much, so I use that drill to train my hands."

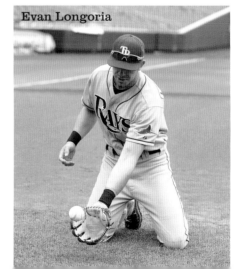

Evan Longoria

After you field a routine ground ball, ideally out in front of your body, the next step is to bring your hands toward the center of your body. From there, shuffle your feet toward the target. That builds momentum for the throw. Your front shoulder should be pointed at the target, and it's important not to cross your feet.

Shuffling toward the target not only builds momentum for the throw, but it also decreases the throw's distance; making a 60-foot toss is easier than a 70-foot one. Use that momentum to complete a strong throw. Arm strength is a function of natural athleticism to some degree, but it's also a product of your mechanics, concentration and practice habits.

Throws should be made with a four-seam grip, with your index and middle fingers across the seams. The idea is to throw the ball straight, making it easy for the first baseman to catch and record the out. Aim for the lettering on the chest of the first baseman's jersey.

On a backhand grab, it's important to stop your momentum from taking you farther away from your target. Plant either foot to stop your momentum, and then push off toward the target. Bring your hands back to the center of your body, turn toward first base and keep your shoulders parallel to the ground while throwing.

Throwing

Pop-ups

The key to effective defense, as every young player is taught, is communication. If you can make the play and have the best angle, call for the ball – loudly. If someone else calls for it and they have a better angle, back off.

Since it's easier to catch a ball in the air by coming in on it, as opposed to moving laterally or backpedaling, the fielder coming forward has priority. When a pop-up is hit between infielders, the shortstop has priority. He has the best angle on most balls, and, if he calls for it, let him have it. (Or take it if you are the shortstop.)

For a pop-up hit between the third baseman and catcher, the third baseman should make the play, since it's much easier to throw to first from his position. The catcher should continue in pursuit until he's called off.

One of the trickier infield plays involves a ball hit behind third base but only slightly down the left-field line. Ideally, the shortstop gets a good jump on the ball – he has the best angle in this situation, and it's his job to call off the third baseman. If the shortstop is unable to get there, he should let the third baseman make the play and communicate with him accordingly. If the play also involves the left fielder, the shortstop has priority over both players.

But it's the left fielder's responsibility to call off the shortstop for balls hit into shallow left field. Still, the shortstop should pursue the play until he is called off.

These situations also unfold on the right side of the field between the second baseman, first baseman and right fielder. The same rules apply, with the right fielder having priority and the second baseman looking to get the best angle.

These guidelines work most of the time for routine plays. But sometimes one fielder gets an especially good (or bad) jump on a ball or an outfielder needs more help from an infielder on a shallow-hit ball. The key, as always, is to communicate.

POSITIONING by
Cristian Guzman

GATHER CLUES

Try to see where the catcher is moving, and get a feel for the batter. Is he strong? Is he favoring one side? That way you can anticipate where a grounder might be hit. The catcher knows where the pitch should go, so watching him — whether he moves inside or outside — can help you a lot.

READ THE BALL

You have to work hard and think fast. If you see a ground ball that's headed your way, it's very important to get a quick read on it. You want to predict how it's going to bounce — long bounce, short bounce, kick bounce — once it gets to you. You should also try to recognize any topspin that the ball might have. You need to keep your head and your body down. See the ball every step of the way. You never know when it can hit a pebble or spin off in a way that you weren't expecting. Don't take your eye off the ball until it is all the way in your glove.

TRANSITION TO THE THROW

You have to keep your legs loose when you're receiving the ball. That makes it easier to get them in position to make a throw in just one or two steps. Once you're throwing, make sure your body is facing your target and that you follow through on the throw.

Rundowns

A rundown looks complicated, but its guidelines are quite simple. When a runner is hung up between bases, everyone on the field should be in motion. Some players will be involved in the play itself, while everyone else should be backing up bases.

The player who initially has the ball charges quickly at the runner, preferably toward the base from which the runner started. That way, if the rundown play fails, the runner has not gained a base. The idea is to get the runner moving quickly. The infielder takes the ball out of his glove and holds it in position to throw. Do *not* pump-fake. This will distract your teammate on the receiving end as much as it will confuse the runner.

Once the runner is moving at top speed, the infielder on the receiving end calls for the ball by yelling, "Now!" The player with the ball should toss it chest high. The player receiving the ball should be sure to catch it before attempting the tag, otherwise a savvy runner could try to knock the ball away.

Your goal is to complete the rundown in just one throw. That's not often the case – many a scorecard includes a crazy notation involving four or five players – but that should be avoided. The more throws involved in the rundown, the greater the potential for error.

After you make the throw, continue running in the direction you were moving. If the rundown continues, you might be next in line to receive a throw and make the out or to keep it going.

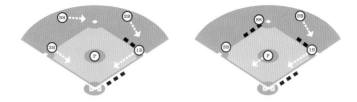

Brooks Robinson, winner of a record 16 Gold Glove Awards at third base, could tell when a batter was getting ready to bunt just by slight changes in his initial stance at the plate. Those bunts were base-hit attempts. Sacrifice bunt attempt situations are much more obvious, as the batter gives away his intention; they usually involve a runner on first base with less than two outs or runners on first and second with no outs.

RUNNER ON FIRST

With a man on first and less than two outs, the first baseman charges as the pitcher delivers. The third baseman charges as the batter squares to bunt. The shortstop covers second base and the second baseman covers first. The goal is to get an out somewhere, preferably at second to eliminate the lead runner. A double play is possible if the ball is bunted directly at someone.

MULTIPLE BASERUNNERS

With runners on first and second, the shortstop covers the bag. The first baseman charges and the second baseman covers first while the pitcher covers the third-base line and the third baseman covers the bag. If the pitcher can't field the ball, the third baseman must leave the bag to make the play. The sacrifice is successful, but the defense's first goal is to get an out – anywhere.

Bunts

A slick-fielding first baseman can be a huge asset to a team, sometimes literally. Big men – such as George Scott, Andres Galarraga, Mark McGwire and Mark Teixeira – have won Gold Glove Awards for their agility around first base.

The key to success at the position is to work on your footwork and on digging balls out of the dirt just as much as you work on your hitting. First basemen are not called upon to cover as much ground as middle infielders, but they're arguably busier than their infield counterparts on every play, between covering first base on

nearly all ground balls, charging on bunt attempts and holding runners on base.

When holding a runner on first, your right foot should be against the base and your left foot up the baseline between first and second. Once the pitcher delivers, you should leave the bag to cover as much ground as possible.

When fielding throws, you should face the direction of the incoming throw. Don't stretch to the bag until the ball is in flight. Keep both of your hands outstretched to receive the ball and make sure that you can move easily to pick a ball from the dirt or reel in an errant throw.

First Base

Second Base

As we've discussed elsewhere in the book, one of a second baseman's key duties is to execute double plays. The quicker you can get to second base, the faster you can set up, and the easier it will be for your teammate to throw to a stationary target.

When you get to the bag, you should put your left foot on it. Your shoulders should be square to the teammate who is throwing to you. Step across the bag with your right foot as you receive the ball and throw to first. It's very important to have your left foot opened straight and pointing toward first. If it's not, and your leg is struck by a sliding runner, a severe knee injury could result.

If the ball is hit at you, use an underhand toss, a backhand toss or a regular throw to make the play to the shortstop who's covering, depending on your proximity to the bag and the nature of the hit. If the ball is hit to you near the bag, you should step on the base with your right foot and throw to first.

Third Base

In many respects, the mechanics of playing third base are similar to those necessary to play other infield positions. Although there are not as many plays at third base as there are at first and second, manning the "hot corner" is a demanding job.

The third baseman sacrifices his body on many plays by blocking hard-hit balls in the dirt – but unlike a catcher, he's not wearing any extra equipment. Fielding a ball down the line and making the long throw across the diamond to first base in time to beat the runner is one of the toughest plays in baseball. It requires quick feet, a back- handed or diving stab of a screeching grounder, a quick recovery and a bullet of a throw to first to record the out.

The third baseman's positioning varies greatly depending on the game situation. With a fast player at the plate, you must protect against the bunt without giving up too much range. You also must occasionally field a bunt or another dribbler bare- handed and make an off-balance throw to first base, a play that looks easy when pulled off by the likes of Big Leaguers such as Evan Longoria and Ryan Zimmerman but is actually much more difficult to execute.

At the youth baseball level, the best athletes are placed at shortstop, a position requiring tremendous speed, great footwork and extended range, not to mention a strong arm. Shortstop has long been the domain of smaller acrobats like Ozzie Smith and Omar Vizquel. But, before transitioning to third base later in their careers, Cal Ripken Jr. and Alex Rodriguez proved that bigger men can play the spot effectively, as well.

The shortstop plays a key role in the double play. You must cheat to double-play depth in any situation when turning two is a possibility. For a ball hit near the bag, you should field the ball and step on the base yourself with your left foot, pushing off the inside of the bag and throwing off your right foot.

In other situations, depending on how far from the bag you field the ball, you can throw it to second using an underhand, sidearm or traditional throw.

For balls hit to the right side of the infield, you become the middle man. You should step hard to second base while facing the player who is throwing the ball. Your right foot should be just next to the bag. As the ball is thrown, move across the base and catch the ball with both hands. Square your left shoulder and make a strong throw to first.

Shortstop

A top-notch defensive pitcher is a huge asset to a team. Instead of being a guy who just falls off the mound, he becomes an effective fifth infielder. Perennial Gold Glove winners like Greg Maddux, Jim Kaat, Bob Gibson and Mike Mussina no doubt won a few games for themselves because of their defensive prowess.

You should not alter your delivery for the sake of getting in better fielding position, though. Pitching effectively is always the top priority, even if it does not result in the best fielding position.

When fielding, bend with your leg, not with your back. Keep the ball in front of your body; don't field it under your body or between your legs. A quick crow hop on the way up can bring some balance and fluidity to your throw to first.

Break toward first base on every ball hit to the right side. Head for a spot about six feet from the base and cut up the foul line so that you're running parallel to the baseline. Shorten your stride as you approach the base in case you have to receive the throw and it is off mark. Touch the inside of the base with your right foot to avoid the runner while making the play.

Pitcher

Tagging

Except in the event of a play at the plate, a tag can be applied with just one hand. When receiving the ball from outfielders or relay men, infielders typically set up in front of the base or straddle it to prepare to put the tag on the incoming runner. Your glove should be out in front of the bag — that way, the runner slides into it, essentially tagging himself. Tags in other situations, like pickoffs and rundowns, also should be applied one-handed.

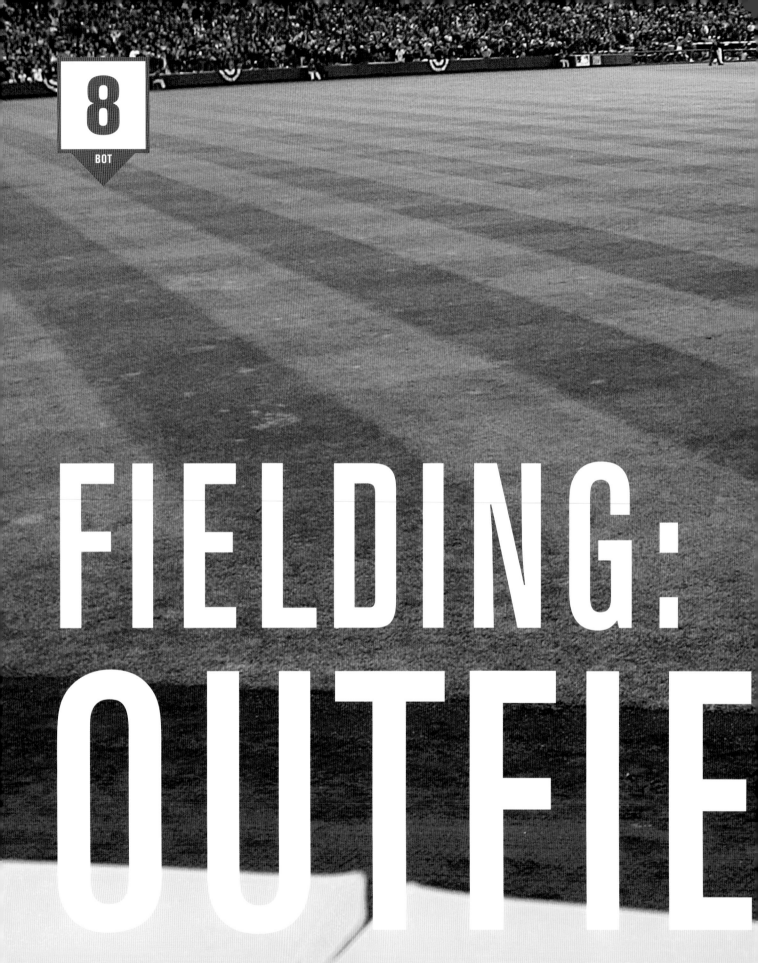

FIELDING: OUTFIE

Approaching fly balls and bouncing balls, throwing and positionin

LDERS

yourself

OUTFIELD DEFENSE IS OFTEN OVERLOOKED at the youth level. The more advanced players usually pitch and play the infield, while the less experienced players are often stashed in the outfield, where fewer balls are hit at that level of play. But that doesn't make outfield positions any less important, at any level.

In high school and beyond, especially, outfield defense often makes the difference between championship-caliber teams and merely very good ones. Some of baseball's greatest all-around athletes — a group that includes Roberto Clemente, Willie Mays, Ken Griffey Jr., Al Kaline, Ichiro Suzuki and Barry Bonds — have won myriad Gold Glove Awards as outfielders.

Diving catches and over-the-fence grabs may be staples of ESPN highlights because great outfielders make even difficult plays look routine by understanding proper positioning and executing sound mechanics to make strong throws, even if they do not possess cannon arms.

"Outfield defense is very underrated," says Bobby Cox, the former Atlanta Braves manager who benefited from having Andruw Jones, a 10-time Gold Glove winner, in center field from 1996–2006. "When you have guys who can cover a lot of ground and make accurate throws, that saves a ton of runs, even if it doesn't always show up in the box score."

Outfielders are a team's last line of defense. Unlike youth baseball, colleges and the professional ranks place some of the best athletes with the strongest arms in the outfield. Dale Murphy moved from catcher and first base to center field, where his athleticism was better utilized, finding his niche and eventually taking home five Gold Gloves in the 1980s.

"You would think you'd be more involved in the game behind the plate or at first, but you move a lot more in the outfield," Murphy said. "They always say it's the outfielders who are the most tired at the end of the game."

The outfield certainly is no place to zone out and pick daisies, even in Tee Ball. It's an outfielder's job to back up a base or a fellow outfielder on *every* play. You must anticipate the ball being hit to you with every swing and have a plan to field the ball and throw accordingly depending on the game situation.

8

Like the Boy Scouts, outfielders operate under the motto "Be Prepared." Your hands should never be on your knees once the pitcher has started his wind-up. Instead, take a step or two forward on the balls of your feet. That puts you in a good athletic position to go in any direction; you can go left or right, drop step and go back, or come forward.

Preparation also involves knowing where you'll throw the ball in any situation – to which base and, if appropriate, which cutoff man. The outfielder should also have an idea of the batter's speed, as well as the speed of any runners on base.

FLY BALLS

Your primary objective, of course, is to catch the ball, and there are ways to get in position once the ball is in the air. You always want to field balls with your momentum coming forward. You never want to make a catch flat-footed or while backpedaling if you can help it. Occasionally a ball will be smashed and you'll have to make an adjustment, but most of the time you can apply the same basic mechanics.

OUTFIELD GROUNDERS

For ground balls to the outfield, you want to take an aggressive pursuit, building momentum as you come forward. If there are no additional runners on base and the ball is hit hard at you, it's okay to drop to a knee for some added insurance against error, but you'll usually want to be in position to come up throwing. For every step you take, the base runner is taking two or three, so move efficiently.

Positioning

Ichiro Suzuki

When a throw is required as part of the play, a right-handed outfielder should field the ball on the outside of his left foot with his head down and his eyes on the ball and come up firing. The reverse applies to left-handed outfielders. If you field the ball on the inside, you risk mishandling the ball or tangling your feet and falling down, which will allow the runners to take extra bases.

"Right before you get to the ball, slow down a little so you're under control," says veteran outfielder Johnny Damon. "Get your feet under you as you field the ball so you're balanced, but also keep your momentum going forward so you can get more on the throw. It's important that you're under control and that the throwing motion is smooth for your entire body."

THE THROW

Take a short crow hop to close off the upper body before you throw. The crow hop gives you some rhythm and builds momentum toward the location of your throw. Without the crow hop, there's a tendency to whip the ball at your target with your arms rather than using the tremendous leverage of your legs to throw.

The crow hop also gives you an extra second to get a good four-seam grip on the ball. Such a grip allows you to throw the ball straight, unlike a two-seam grip that will cut or slice.

Another way to envision the crow hop is to think about gaining ground toward the target. You do this by squaring the instep of your throwing-side foot to the target at which you're throwing. As you step and bring your hands to the spot where the ball and glove separate, your upper body will turn, closing your front shoulder so that it's pointed toward the target, aligning you for the throw.

While everyone would like to have a cannon like Roberto Clemente's, Ichiro's or Vladimir Guerrero's, most outfielders must get by in the outfield with average arms. Proper positioning and fundamentals can compensate.

"I never had a great throwing arm, so I worked hard on everything else," says Hall of Famer Tony Gwynn, who won five Gold Glove Awards with the Padres before becoming the head baseball coach at San Diego State. "If you charge a ball hard, you're shortening the distance you have to throw, and that's going to give you more of a chance to throw guys out."

THROWING FROM THE OUTFIELD
by Torii Hunter

SNEAK A PEEK

Before the ball is hit, you've got to know what you're going to do with it once you catch it. Right before the ball is in your glove, peek and see if the runner is tagging up or going halfway. If he tags up, you'd better make a quick throw to the next base. If he goes halfway, you've got to hit the cutoff man.

ANTICIPATE

I know there can be times, especially in Little League, when there are hardly any balls hit to you. But stay focused. What I do is anticipate. I start focusing on the pitcher — if he's throwing the ball inside, I might scoot over to my right, knowing a right-handed hitter likely will pull the ball, or if he's throwing the ball away, I go to my left. Play the mind game, and have fun with it. Baseball is a fun game, so enjoy yourself.

THINK ON YOUR FEET

When the ball is hit, the first thing you've got to think is, "Where is that ball going to land?" Then you've got to run right to that spot. The quickest way to get there is a straight line. You can practice this by having a friend throw the ball to your right and left, and running straight to that spot. You know who can hit the ball far and who can't. If you think the hitter is going to hit the ball over your head, get ready to run toward the ball. If he's less powerful, be ready to run in. Don't play the same way for every hitter.

Fly Balls

As with fielding grounders, the goal of catching fly balls is to set yourself up to throw quickly. It's important to position yourself behind the ball to gain momentum going forward after the catch.

MAKING THE CATCH

Always try to catch the ball with two hands to ensure that you complete the catch, even after you've gained experience. But whether a ball is caught with one hand or two, it's important that the glove remains above your eyes, so that you can see the ball into your glove and block the sun, which will be discussed later in this section. If the glove is below your eyes, you're going to have to take your eye off the ball before you make the grab, and even a split second is enough for you to lose track of the ball.

Letting the ball travel below your field of vision increases the possibility of your misjudging it – or even getting hit in the head. That is what once happened to Jose Canseco, when a ball hit him on the head and bounced over the fence for a home run.

If you have to run to catch the ball, catch it with one hand. In most situations, you should have time to run to a spot about 10 feet behind where the ball will come down. That way you will be able to build momentum coming forward to make a strong throw.

GOING BACK

Many fly balls are anything but routine. The most difficult skill for you to learn as an outfielder is how to go back on those balls hit over your head.

When you go back on a ball, you should never backpedal; instead, use a drop step – to your right when the ball is hit over your right shoulder and to your left when it's hit over your left shoulder. Once you make the drop step, cross over and pursue the ball while running back at an angle. In this position, you have much more speed and a better angle on the ball than you would if you were backpedaling, an approach which compromises your balance and ability to jump. As always, your goal is to get behind the ball and make the catch with your momentum propelling you forward.

When learning the drop step, it's important to stay focused on the ball. When you're running at top speed, there's a natural tendency for your eyes to wander. A great way to work on maintaining focus is with the quarterback drill, in which a coach or parent plays the role of quarterback, throwing balls over your head. The goal of the drill, which is described in detail at the end of the book, is to learn to focus on the ball as you run hard and see the ball into your glove.

But what if the ball is hit so hard that you won't be in position to follow it? In this variation of the drill, the ball is thrown with more force. Take off like a sprinter, with your head down and your arms to the side. After taking five or six steps, peek over your shoulder and find the ball, then run to the spot to make the catch. Don't turn your whole body, because you might tangle your feet.

BLOCKING THE SUN

The toughest play for an outfielder is to catch a ball that's been hit into the glare of the sun. In that situation, you have to use a combination of sunglasses, your glove and even the bill of your hat to track the ball. Do not look directly into the sun, even though it's instinctual to do so if you're following the path of the ball. If you do, you will temporarily blind yourself, and you'll be less likely to make the play.

On sunny days, make it a point to practice shielding your eyes from the sun with your glove in between innings. As the ball reaches the top of its arc, use your glove to shade your eyes until you can see the ball on its way down. Getting a side angle on the ball can also help you to see it better on its descent. Once you get a beat on the ball, it's business as usual. Get behind it and make the catch with your momentum coming forward.

Catching balls in the sun is not practiced nearly enough, as many teams hold practices late in the afternoon when the sun is setting. It's also difficult for even an experienced fungo hitter to place the ball correctly. Coaches should practice this by tossing a ball 30 feet in the air and throwing it progressively higher from there.

No matter how well you position yourself in the outfield, there will be balls hit too well for you to catch in the air or field on the ground with your momentum coming forward. For shots hit into the gaps or the corners, it's imperative that you be ready to adapt to the game situation and minimize the damage.

COMMUNICATE

Communication is vital. Some of baseball's worst injuries occur when outfielders collide while running at top speed. On balls hit to one of the gaps, the outfielder with the shortest angle should be able to dive for it with confidence, knowing that another outfielder is running a deeper angle and backing him up should he miss.

The center fielder has priority on all balls hit to the outfield and should call the corner outfielders off loudly and repeatedly if he can make the play.

It's your job as an outfielder to make all of the plays you can so that you do not put pressure on the infielders to make an acrobatic catch on a bloop hit. Here, too, communication is the key to avoiding collisions. It's important that all players maintain good communication and that someone makes the catch. There's nothing worse than when a catchable ball drops for a base hit due to a lack of interaction.

It's never a good idea to dive straight ahead for balls, though, since you risk injuring your wrist or breaking your collarbone by doing so – it's better to attempt a sliding catch in those situations.

IN THE CORNER

Few teams work enough on fielding balls hit to the corners. Outfielders should practice fielding the ball and making strong throws to second, third and home, hitting the proper cutoff man and keeping the ball on a low trajectory. Such drills, with outfielders lined up near the corners and a coach smashing fungos, are great ways to work on relay plays and to strengthen the last line of defense.

Tough Plays

CATCHING FLY BALLS
by Bernie Williams

GET UNDER IT

If it's coming your way, you should get under the ball and line it up right between your eyes, with both hands high above your head. At this point, keep a space between your glove and your bare hand so that you don't block your view of the ball. As the ball is coming down, move your glove in front of your face, still high above your head, and keep your elbows slightly bent. You should now place your bare hand on the back of the webbing to guide the ball into your glove. Then, as the baseball drops into your glove, all you have to do is squeeze.

PRACTICE, PRACTICE, PRACTICE

How well you judge fly balls in the outfield has a lot to do with instincts. The more you practice, the better your instincts will become. You have to practice catching fly balls every chance you get in order to improve.

BE ON YOUR TOES

Now it's time to concentrate on how you position yourself. Be relaxed, place your feet about shoulder-width apart and bend your knees slightly. It's important to put your weight on the balls (front) of your feet. That will prepare you to move in any direction. If you're sitting back on your heels, you won't be able to react quickly.

RULEBOOK BASICS

Examining some of baseball's rules

IN THE 1980s, A SERIES of two-part football commercials titled "You Make the Call" debuted. Viewers saw footage from a close, unusual NFL play and were given two options to make the call on their own. The viewers then got to ponder their decisions during a commercial break for the sponsor of the segment. When the commercial break ended, the correct call was revealed.

Baseball can be just as complex as football when it comes to rules, some of which don't arise often in game situations. While the *Official Rules of Major League Baseball* governs the Big Leagues, other levels of baseball maintain their own guidelines. The most common rules, though, are applicable to all of baseball, no matter the level of play. Having a good understanding of the rules that apply to your league — even the unusual ones — is important for any coach or player. Not only does such knowledge diffuse arguments between coaches and umpires, many of which are disputes regarding rules interpretations, but it also can give your team a better chance of winning. After all, a team that has mastered the intricacies of the rule book will have an advantage over its opponents.

There are numerous rules interpretations that are likely to come up over the course of a season. What follows in this chapter are some of baseball's more prominent ones.

Balk

No matter the level of play, when a pitcher makes a move away from the plate with runners on base, someone in the crowd is bound to yell, "Balk!" even if the pitcher has executed a textbook pick-off move.

That's because few fans and non-pitchers ever take the time to peruse Section 8.05 of the rule book, which addresses more than a dozen factors that determine whether an umpire will call a pitcher for a balk, an infraction that gives runners an extra base. Most balks occur with a fast runner on first base, when the pitcher, in an attempt to confuse the runner, does not come to a full stop in the stretch position before either throwing to first or to the plate.

The balk is an unusual call in the Majors, where pitchers have honed their pick-off moves over many years. At the youth level, though, balks can be more commonplace. That's why coaches should understand the rule and work with pitchers to prevent balks.

Right-handed pitchers should learn to turn off the rubber with their right foot, plant with their left foot toward first and make the quick throw to the base. The best way to avoid committing a balk is to master the comfortable stretch position and remain calm, regardless of how fast the runner may be. One way to deter aggressive runners is simply to vary the amount of time you hold onto the ball.

Umpires spend a lot of time in umpiring school learning the balk play. When they see a balk, they're taught to point at the pitcher and yell, "That's a balk! Time!"

The umpire should throw both hands in the air, point at the runner and then signal to the proceeding base. The purpose of this routine is not just to sell the call, but also to be as definitive as possible before making the call.

Infield Fly

An infield fly, according to the *Official Rules of Major League Baseball*, is "a fair fly ball (not including a line drive nor an attempted bunt) which can be caught by any infielder with ordinary effort, when first and second bases – or first, second and third – are occupied with fewer than two outs. The pitcher, catcher and any outfielder who stations himself in the infield on the play shall be considered infielders for the purpose of this rule."

By yelling, "Infield fly!" – usually while waving his arms – the umpire automatically rules the batter out, even if the ball is not caught. At the youth level, the umpire sometimes will yell, "Infield fly – batter's out," to clarify his call for the players.

The purpose of the infield fly rule is to maintain fairness. When a ball is popped up in the infield, the runners assume that it will be caught and therefore stay on the base. If no infield fly rule existed, the fielder could deliberately allow the ball to drop, forcing the runners to advance. In that situation, they'd likely be part of a double play, or even a triple play, because they lingered too long on the base before advancing. This differs from a fly ball to the outfield, when a runner can go halfway to the next base and have time to get back to the bag safely if the ball is caught.

When a potential infield fly occurs, the umpire rules whether the ball could have ordinarily been handled by an infielder – not just within some arbitrary limitation such as the grass or the base lines. The umpire must also rule that a ball is an infield fly, even when handled by an outfielder, if, in the umpire's judgment, the ball could have been just as easily handled by an infielder. The infield fly is not considered an appeal play. The umpire's judgment must govern, and the decision to call an infield fly should be made immediately.

Interference and Obstruction

Interference is a broad rule book term that refers to a number of illegal actions that occur during a contest to change the course of the game. Interference can be committed by the team at the plate or the team in the field, as well as by a player not even in the game at the time, an umpire, a fan or another individual not associated with the team.

One key distinction between interference and obstruction: Interference is a defined as a violation by either the offense or the defense; obstruction is classified as a violation by the defense alone.

OFFENSIVE INTERFERENCE

Offensive interference is the most common infraction and refers, according to the *Official Rules of Major League Baseball*, to "an act by the team at bat which interferes with, obstructs, impedes, hinders or confuses any fielder attempting to make a play." An umpire can call a batter, batter-runner or runner out for offensive interference when he engages in any of the above behavior against the defensive team, sending any other runner to the last base that the umpire determines he occupied before the call was made.

CATCHER'S INTERFERENCE

Catcher's interference occurs when the catcher interferes with the batter's ability to hit a pitch. This happens when the batter swings and strikes the catcher's glove or a portion of the catcher's body, usually during steal attempts when the catcher has inched too close to the batter in order to prepare to make a throw. When catcher's interference is called, the batter is awarded first base. Those runners on base who are forced by the batter to advance are also awarded the next bag. If a runner had been attempting to steal, he is safe.

FAN INTERFERENCE

Spectator interference occurs when a fan or another individual not associated with the team — such as a bullpen attendant or a batboy — alters a play in progress. Such interference most typically occurs on foul balls hit into the first row of the stands that a fielder would have had a chance to catch if the fan did not prevent him from doing so.

Whether such incidents are deemed interference depends on whether the umpire determines that fielder could have caught the ball over the field of play. If the fielder reaches into the stands and is hindered in making a catch, no interference is called. If the fan reaches over the railing and thwarts the fielder's attempt at a play, interference is called. The umpire will award any outs or bases depending on what he believes would have transpired had the interference not occurred.

OBSTRUCTION

Obstruction is the act of a fielder who, while not in possession of the ball and not in the act of fielding it, impedes the progress of any runner on the basepaths.

According to the *Official Rules of Major League Baseball*, "If a fielder is about to receive a thrown ball and if the ball is in flight directly toward and near enough to the fielder so that he must occupy his position to receive the ball, he may be considered 'in the act of fielding a ball.'" The umpire may use his discretion to determine if a fielder is engaged in such an act. A player is no longer considered to be actively fielding a batted ball after he has made an unsuccessful attempt to do so, and any conduct that impedes an offensive player after such an attempt qualifies as obstruction of that runner.

Rule 7.08(f) states that any runner is out when he is touched by a fair batted ball in fair territory before the ball has touched or passed an infielder.

"That rule is in the rule book for a reason – when a ball is in an area where a fielder could field it, and it hits a runner while the fielder is behind him to make the play, then he's out," says longtime MLB umpire Jerry Layne. "But if a fielder has had an opportunity to field the ball, and it hits the runner and there's no other fielder behind him, then it's nothing. So, the only time a runner in the infield is ever protected from being hit by a ball is if there's been an opportunity for somebody to field it and nobody's behind him, or if it's an infield fly, which is a pop-up, and it hits him while he's standing on the bag."

Balls That Hit a Runner

A batter is only out on strikes once the catcher legally catches the third strike. This guideline can be found in Rule 6.05(b) and dates back to the early days of baseball. The exception to this rule is Rule 6.09(b) and occurs when first base is unoccupied with less than two outs.

As a batter, you should be aware of these rules, since they might give you a second chance at safely reaching base. Instead of just walking back to the dugout after a strikeout when first base is open, double check to make sure the catcher caught the ball. Of course, you can do this even with a man on first, as long as there are two outs.

On a dropped third strike with the bases loaded and two outs, all the catcher needs to do is tag or step on home plate for the out. Rule 6.09(b) states that the batter becomes a runner when a third strike is not caught with first base unoccupied or with first base occupied and two outs. A force can be made at any base when the batter becomes a runner with the bases loaded.

Dropped Third Strikes

Batting Out of Order

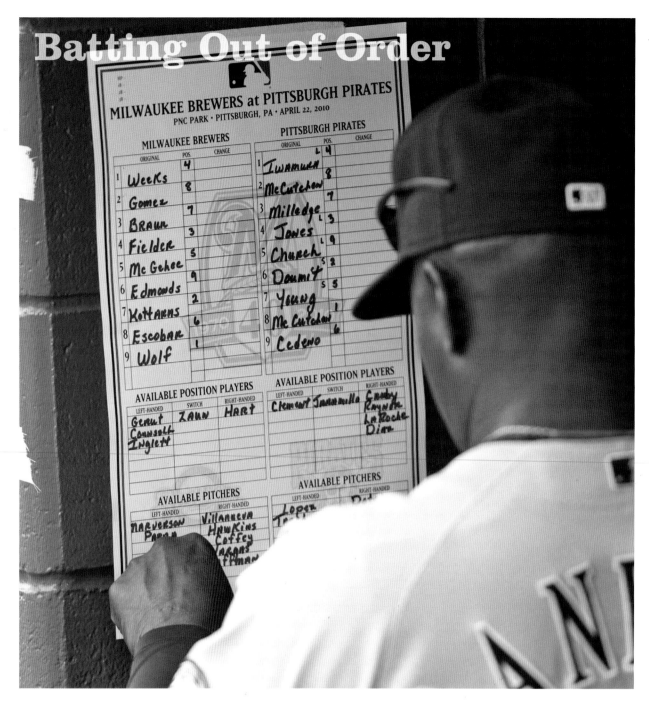

MILWAUKEE BREWERS at PITTSBURGH PIRATES
PNC PARK · PITTSBURGH, PA · APRIL 22, 2010

MILWAUKEE BREWERS

ORIGINAL	POS.	CHANGE
1 Weeks	4	
2 Gomez	8	
3 Braun	7	
4 Fielder	3	
5 McGehee	5	
6 Edmonds	9	
7 Kottahns	2	
8 Escobar	6	
9 Wolf	1	

PITTSBURGH PIRATES

ORIGINAL	POS.	CHANGE
1 Iwamura	4	
2 McCutchen	8	
3 Milledge	7	
4 Jones	3	
5 Church	9	
6 Doumit	2	
7 Young	5	
8 McCutchen	1	
9 Cedeno	6	

AVAILABLE POSITION PLAYERS

LEFT-HANDED	SWITCH	RIGHT-HANDED
Gerut Counsell Inglett	Zaun	Hart

AVAILABLE POSITION PLAYERS

LEFT-HANDED	SWITCH	RIGHT-HANDED
Clement Jaramillo		Crosby Raynor LaRoche Diaz

AVAILABLE PITCHERS

LEFT-HANDED		RIGHT-HANDED
Narverson Parra		Villanueva Hawkins Coffey Jaramo Hoffman

AVAILABLE PITCHERS

LEFT-HANDED		RIGHT-HANDED
Lopez Taschner		

It's the responsibility of the defensive team, not the umpire, to notice when a team has batted out of order. Contrary to popular belief, an out is called on the batter who was supposed to have hit, not the one who actually did.

Suppose Rickie Weeks leads off for Milwaukee and flies out. Ryan Braun – penciled into the Brewers batting order in the third spot – then bats out of turn in the No. 2 hole, hitting a double. Before a pitch is thrown to the next batter, a member of the defensive team asks the umpire to make a ruling. The defensive team must wait until *after* the incorrect hitter's at-bat to appeal so that he is guaranteed an out; if the issue is mentioned before the at-bat has ended, the hitter is replaced.

Since the proper batter after Weeks was Carlos Gomez and not Braun, Gomez is called out for failing to bat. Braun is removed from second base and his double is negated, but he comes to bat again, since he is now the proper batter.

Appeal Play

An appeal play takes place when a member of the team in the field calls the attention of an umpire to an infraction he might otherwise have missed during the course of play.

Appeals question whether a runner tagged properly, touched a base the last time he passed or touched all bases in order. To make an appeal, an infielder must have a live ball – thrown to him by the pitcher – and must tag the runner or base in question and inform the umpire of the infraction and which runner committed it. The umpire then issues a ruling on the matter.

Because appeals are the responsibility of the defensive team, it's important that fielders and coaches make sure to watch everything that is happening on the field, as they cannot expect an umpire to rule in their favor without initiating an appeal.

One of the great things about baseball is the opportunity to witness something that has never happened before. Even though the game has been played for well over a century, situations still occur in the game when there is no applicable rule.

One memorable example occurred in a 2001 Spring Training game in Tucson, Ariz. Randy Johnson, pitching for the Diamondbacks against the San Francisco Giants, unleashed a fastball at the very moment that a dove flew in front of home plate. The ball struck the bird, which flew over catcher Rod Barajas's head and landed a few feet from the plate amid a sea of feathers.

Bizarre plays such as this are not covered in the *Official Rules*. When a situation that is not included in the book arises during a contest, Rule 9.01(c) comes into play. This rule gives an umpire the authority to make a judgment call on any point not specifically mentioned in the rule book. In such instances, the umpire is instructed to use common sense and fair play. In the Giants-Diamondbacks game, the umpires called it no pitch, and the count remained the same, as precedent could not dictate otherwise.

When There is No Rule

DEVELOPING TALENT

Helping players improve

WHEN KIDS ARE PLAYING TEE Ball or their first few years of organized baseball, an emphasis is placed on learning the game and mastering the fundamentals. The goal of this book has been to provide a framework and an overview for how to do just that.

For many kids, baseball is nothing more than a way to enjoy a few spring and summer afternoons and evenings, competing in a wondrous game that has been passed down through the generations.

For others, baseball becomes a year-round pastime at an early age. Kids in this situation advance quickly into playing for traveling teams and in multiple leagues, sometimes as early as age 8. Some parlay their experience into playing in college or, in some rare instances, the professional ranks.

Such one-sport specialization has largely developed during the last 15 years. It's extremely rare to see an athlete like Hall of Famer Dave Winfield, who was drafted by three professional leagues — the NFL, the NBA and Major League Baseball — or even someone like Carl Crawford, who was offered Division I college scholarships to play all three of those sports.

It's a little more common to see ballplayers with similarities to Atlanta Braves outfielder Jason Heyward, who, despite being a 6-foot-5, 240-pound man, never played football and only briefly dabbled in basketball, concentrating on baseball year-round since he was 8 years old.

Carl Crawford   Jason Heyward

9
BOT

293

Specialization

Athletic trainers suggest that young athletes should play a number of sports to develop a wide range of their movement patterns. Several Big Leaguers hold a similar mindset.

"I'm a firm believer in playing at least two sports," says former Braves pitcher Tom Glavine, who was a good enough hockey player to have been drafted by the NHL's Los Angeles Kings in 1984. "It helps you develop multiple sets of skills, and it keeps you from getting burned out on any one sport."

Involvement in multiple sports also prevents the type of overuse injuries commonly seen in baseball, specifically those suffered as a result of too much pitching. In his book *Until it Hurts: America's Obsession with Youth Sports and How it Harms Our Kids*, author Mark Hyman writes about parents who have turned youth sports into high-pressure, big-money enterprises at the expense of their children's well-being. Hyman explains how he pushed his son to pitch too often, and, as a result, his son developed arm problems.

LET THEM PLAY

In previous generations, kids played baseball and other sports informally after school on sandlots and in backyards. Most kids now grow up knowing only organized sports. The culture of scheduling and specialization has created a pre-professional sports blueprint for parents to follow.

"In the '60s and '70s, there was not this gold rush mentality with scholarships and playing professionally," Hyman says. "Now parents pay big money for private coaching, travel teams and medical bills, all with the idea of the kid getting into the college of their parents' choice, preferably with a scholarship."

Jimmy Rollins

9

Mike Piazza

Anthony Rao, a child psychologist and the author of *The Way of Boys: Raising Healthy Boys in a Challenging and Complex World*, suggests that the epidemic of attention deficit hyperactivity disorder is due in part to many youngsters not getting enough exercise beyond organized sports.

"It's the cutest thing in the world to see little kids trying to hit a ball on a tee, but other than giving them the basics of what baseball is, they're not getting a lot of physical activity," Rao says. "They're waiting around trying to hit this thing at the end of a pipe, and it's too much of a parent involvement thing. There are too many of them hovering around not letting kids come up with their own rules and solutions to problems, be with kids of different ages, learn the skills and let their bodies move in a natural way."

On the other hand, many year-round programs emphasize core conditioning and the types of injury-preventative training regimens that were foreign to ballplayers just a generation ago. For those kids looking to master a skill in 10,000 hours the way Malcolm Gladwell chronicles in his best-selling book, *Outliers*, there is the opportunity to participate in all-encompassing programs throughout the country.

Lastings Milledge

For some youngsters, just the task of finding a place to play for part of the year can be a challenge because of their locations and economic factors.

RBI

The Reviving Baseball in Inner Cities (RBI) program presented by KPMG was created in 1989 by former Big Leaguer John Young with the goal of reintroducing baseball to inner-city children – many of whom increasingly were turning to football and basketball – and keeping kids out of trouble.

Since 1989, it has grown from a local program for boys in South Central Los Angeles to a wide-reaching endeavor that serves more than 200 cities and as many as 100,000 male and female players annually.

RBI, which has been under the MLB umbrella since 1991 and is run in conjunction with Boys & Girls Clubs of America, is part of baseball's multi-pronged approach to rekindling baseball interest among African-American kids from underprivileged neighborhoods.

Young noticed that many baseball leagues had become undermanned and underfunded at the time, and his solution was RBI, a comprehensive youth program that would encourage baseball participation and expand the talent pool. The program would also provide youngsters with a team-oriented activity that would keep them occupied and off the streets.

MLB provided financial support for RBI, as did the Los Angeles Dodgers, the City of Los Angeles and professional services firm KPMG. MLB has invested more than $30 million in RBI since its inception. With the program growing, Young has stressed an academic component to RBI, fostering educational and social skills through athletic competition while teaching kids the importance of accountability and community responsibility.

ALTERNATE PATH

The RBI program has provided a path for many of its alumni to enter the college and professional ranks, with more than 170 former RBI participants having been drafted by Major League clubs since the program's inception. RBI alumni in the Majors include Carl Crawford, Jimmy Rollins, CC Sabathia, Coco Crisp, Lastings Milledge, Yovani Gallardo, James Loney and Justin Upton.

For many players, RBI leagues provide an organized place to showcase their talents that they might not otherwise receive.

"Options were limited for a guy like me to be seen by Major League scouts," says Crawford, who grew up in Houston. "RBI allowed me to be seen by a group of people who normally wouldn't have seen me."

James Loney

Coco Crisp

Justin Upton

Inner-city Baseball

CC Sabathia

Luis Gonzalez

INCLUSIVE OPPORTUNITY

Although the RBI program is often associated with minority children, it benefits kids from all demographics. With youth baseball in many parts of the country increasingly becoming the domain of year-round travel teams and private clinics, the sport can be as elite an activity as golf.

Toronto Blue Jays pitcher Jesse Litsch understood that his father, Rick, who raised him alone, couldn't afford $1,000 travel team fees. So Jesse played in the St. Petersburg (Fla.) RBI chapter instead, competing in the shadow of Tampa Bay's Tropicana Field. Some days, he would finish an RBI practice or game and head straight to the ballpark, where he served as a bat boy and clubhouse attendant for the Big League club.

Jesse Litsch

Steve Garvey

"Baseball has become an expensive sport, and RBI provides kids with a great opportunity," says Litsch. "There lots of kids that don't get scouted these days. But college coaches and pro scouts need to check out the RBI programs. You can find a lot of diamonds in the rough."

BASEBALL CLIMATES

Year-round baseball, though more commonplace in recent years, is not a new phenomenon. In warmer climates such as Florida and Southern California, kids have been playing baseball year-round for decades. Not surprisingly, those regions have produced an abundance of professionals and college players.

The Tampa, Fla., area alone has produced a slew of players, including Hall of Famers Al Lopez and Wade Boggs, as well as Fred McGriff, Steve Garvey, Dwight Gooden, Brad Radke, Lou Piniella, Gary Sheffield, Luis Gonzalez, Kenny Rogers, Chone Figgins and Chris Coghlan.

"I think scouts come to see you in games there because they know a lot of kids come out of that area," says Red Sox hitting coach and former Big Leaguer Dave Magadan, a Tampa native.

Jeff Francoeur

On the Fast Track

Brian McCann

Corey Patterson

These days, talented young players have the option of enrolling at places like the IMG Academies, year-round residential sports complexes where athletes train and go to school. The baseball academy at IMG is modeled after the famous Bollettieri Tennis Academy, which IMG purchased in 1987 and expanded into other sports.

There's also East Cobb Baseball, which was created in the northern Atlanta suburbs in 1985, not long after a team from Marietta, Ga., won the Little League World Series. Guerry Baldwin, a Pony League coach in Marietta, thought it made sense for players to be grouped together based on ability rather than age or home address. A wealthy benefactor helped build a 30-acre, eight-field complex that has since become the most prominent year-round facility in the country, producing such Big Leaguers as Jason Heyward, Brian McCann, Jeff Francoeur and Corey Patterson.

Eugene Heyward, Jason's father, spent as many as six hours a day in the car during his son's childhood shuttling between home, work and the East Cobb complex. Eugene and Laura Heyward admit that such year-round specialization is not for everyone, but the opportunity is there for kids who want it.

"It's really up to the person, the kid," Laura Heyward says. "Do they want to do it? Are they having fun?"

Mark Reynolds

Players are evaluated at every level of baseball. Anyone with college or professional potential will likely be seen by scouts during his high school career. If such a college opportunity presents itself, the key is to choose a school based not on the team, possible playing opportunities or other baseball-related concerns – it's more important to make your decision based on the quality of education you'll receive. That's because only a select few players will have a chance to pursue professional baseball as a career.

ANYTHING CAN HAPPEN
Even then, there are no guarantees. Two of baseball's

best third basemen were not viewed as professional prospects until well into their college careers. Ryan Zimmerman, who grew up playing in southeastern Virginia with the likes of the Upton brothers and Mark Reynolds, received just one Division I scholarship – to the University of Virginia, which had a long-struggling baseball program until Zimmerman and Reynolds turned it into a national contender.

Evan Longoria didn't receive any college scholarship offers coming out of high school and attended community college for a year before enrolling at California's Long Beach State. Eric Karros was a walk-on player at UCLA. His one-time Dodgers

teammate, Mike Piazza, was a 62nd-round draft pick. Even 2009 No. 1 draft pick Stephen Strasburg was not deemed a prospect when he first arrived at San Diego State in 2006.

LEVEL PLAYING FIELD
An important lesson to reinforce to kids is that baseball can be pursued at many different levels. Even for the most promising youngsters, there are no guarantees. But between year-round programs and a scouting world that has become increasingly accessible because of the Internet, opportunities abound for hard-working players to compete at the next level, whatever that might be.

Ryan Zimmerman

Eric Karros

Professional Aspirations

Evan Longoria

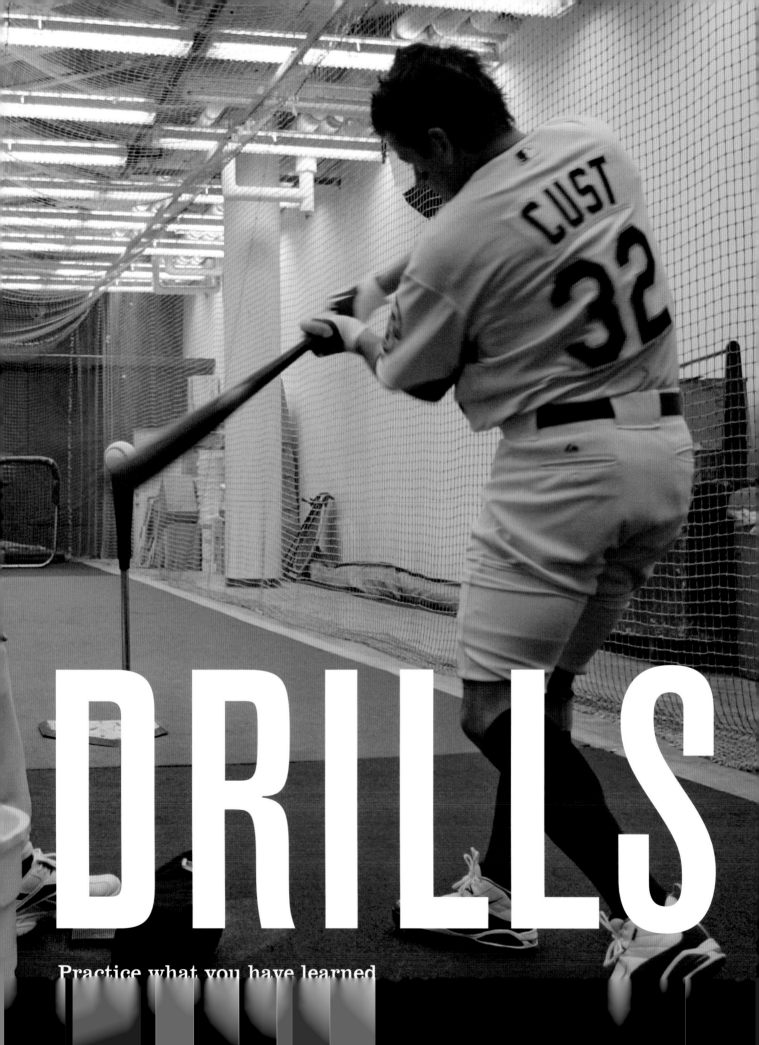

DRILLS

Practice what you have learned

DRILL:
ELBOW THROWS

IMPROVES:
GRIP, WRISTS

EXECUTION:
Get on one knee about six feet away from your partner.

Bend your elbow up and hold your forearm with your other hand.

Hold the ball using the proper four-seam grip, bend your wrist back and flick the ball to your partner's glove, making sure to only use your wrist on the throw.

Once you're comfortable, back up gradually until you're 15 feet away from your partner and repeat.

DRILL:
ONE-KNEE THROWS

IMPROVES:
UPPER-BODY THROWING MECHANICS

EXECUTION:
Get on one knee about 15 feet away from your partner.

Rotate your front shoulder toward your target and bring your throwing arm behind you, with your hand on top of the ball.

Make sure you have a proper grip on the ball, use a circular arm motion and throw using both your elbow and wrist.

DRILL:
LONG-TOSS

IMPROVES:
ARM STRENGTH

EXECUTION:
Form two lines of paired-up players.

Start 10 yards away from your partner. Throw the ball back and forth.

If the ball does not hit the ground, move back several steps. Continue to move back, making strong, accurate throws, until you can no longer throw normally, without an arc.

DRILL:
KNEE LIFT

IMPROVES:
BALANCE

EXECUTION:

Starting in the set position, lift your front knee and hold the position for several seconds.

Drop your knee and move into your stride.

Complete your normal pitching motion, controlling your direction toward home plate.

DRILL:
3/4-POSITION

IMPROVES:
RELEASE POINT

EXECUTION:

Spread your feet slightly wider than shoulder-width apart with the toes of your lead leg pointing to your target.

Assume the 3/4-position, with the elbow of both arms level with your shoulders. Your glove arm should be pointed at the catcher and bent down, with your glove facing the ground. Your throwing arm should be bent up, with the ball in the air.

Pull your glove arm back to your body while rotating your hips. Pivot on your back foot before you release the ball, but keep your back foot in contact with the ground throughout the drill.

Bend your back and bring your throwing-arm elbow to your opposite knee to follow through.

DRILL:
BUCKET DRILL

IMPROVES:
FOLLOW-THROUGH

EXECUTION:

Pair up with a partner and kneel on your leg on the same side as your throwing arm.

Place the toes of your kneeling foot on an upside-down bucket, with the bottom of your foot facing upward.

Rotate your shoulder toward your partner, bring your arm back and throw the ball.

As you throw, pop up to a standing position and bring your upper body over your stride leg, finishing the throw with your elbow past your opposite knee.

DRILL:
PITCHING ACCURACY

IMPROVES:
COMMAND

EXECUTION:

Place four cones between home plate and second base – the first will be halfway between home and the pitcher's mound, the second 3/4 of the way, the third on the mound and the fourth between the mound and second base.

Starting at the first cone, throw 10 pitches to the catcher, who will act as an umpire and count balls and strikes.

If you reach 10 pitches before throwing four balls, move back to the next cone.

Keep moving back until the last cone, throwing three balls or fewer out of the strike zone at each distance.

DRILL:
DOT SPOT

IMPROVES:
COMMAND

EXECUTION:

Place four circles of different colors on the catcher's equipment – one on each knee and one on each shoulder.

The coach should announce a color designating the location for each pitch.

Using the dots as targets, the pitcher should throw the ball to the correct spot, and the catcher should catch each pitch thrown to him.

DRILL:
FIRST-BASE PICKOFFS

IMPROVES:
PICK-OFF MOVES

EXECUTION:

Position four pitchers on the mound, each facing a base or home plate, with a coach standing in the middle.

Station two players at each base to act as a first baseman and a base runner, respectively.

On the coach's direction, either pick off the runner at the base corresponding to the position in which you are standing on the mound or simulate a pitch to home plate.

Practice disguising your pick-off move for the runners, who will be attempting to steal.

DRILL:
PITCHER'S LAUNCH

IMPROVES:
DELIVERY

EXECUTION:

Position yourself on the mound with your feet shoulder-width apart, your back foot parallel to the rubber and your front foot angled toward home plate.

Initiate the throw by transferring your weight to your back leg.

Move your arms into a position so that your glove arm is bent down with your elbow pointing at the target and your throwing arm is bent up at a 90-degree angle behind your body with your elbow level with your shoulder.

Rotate your torso toward the target, bringing your glove hand palm-up into your armpit.

Follow through with your throwing arm, releasing the ball and letting your back leg come forward.

DRILL:
LEVERAGE

IMPROVES:
STAYING TALL, SPEED BEHIND THE PITCH

EXECUTION:

Start in a position with your feet together and parallel to the rubber.

Bend your back leg slightly while bringing your front knee up, as you would in your delivery.

Have a coach measure the height of your knee in this position and place a piece of tape on your body at that height.

Return to your original position and begin your delivery, staying tall on your back leg so that your front knee reaches the same height.

Simulate a pitch to home plate. As you progress, add a baseball and complete the throw.

DRILL:
STRIDE

IMPROVES:
STRIDE LENGTH

EXECUTION:

Stand perpendicular to a straight line, like a foul line in the outfield. Mark your starting point.

Laying down with your feet on the same starting point, measure your height along the line, and place an object in that spot in the direction that you will be throwing.

Go through your delivery, striding parallel to the foul line.

Check to see where your front foot lands in relation to the object. For maximum velocity, your front foot should land at or beyond the object marking the length of your height.

DRILL:

BATTING PRACTICE WITH HIPS FOCUS

IMPROVES:

HIP ROTATION, BALANCE

EXECUTION:

Assume your normal stance and place a bat behind your back (parallel to the ground), holding it with both arms between your biceps and forearm.

Have a partner simulate a wind-up and deliver an imaginary pitch.

Your partner should yell "inside" or "outside" as he delivers the pitch.

Coil as you normally would, stride and then rotate your hips open.

Open your hips further on an inside pitch than an outside pitch.

Make sure that you pivot your back foot to drive your hip rotation.

DRILL:

HITTING FROM A TEE

IMPROVES:

STANCE, WEIGHT TRANSFER, STRIDE

EXECUTION:

Set the tee to a comfortable height.

Start by placing a ball on the tee in the middle of the plate, thigh-high.

Take several swings at the tee.

Move the tee forward and in to simulate an inside pitch. Move the tee back and outside to simulate an outside pitch.

Vary the height of the tee at each position to simulate high and low pitches.

Practice staying in the same hitting position every time and executing the same stride and follow-through.

DRILL:

SOFT-TOSS

IMPROVES:

QUICK WRISTS

EXECUTION:

Grab a partner and have him toss you balls from a kneeling position on the side and in front of you. You will be hitting into a net or fence for this drill.

The tosser should feed you good throws at a fairly quick pace, varying the height and position of each throw to simulate different types of pitches.

Concentrate on keeping your head down and leading with the knob of the bat while making adjustments to each toss.

DRILL:
VISION DRILL

IMPROVES:
PITCH IDENTIFICATION

EXECUTION:

Color a bunch of baseballs entirely or between the inside seams, and assign each color a different action (i.e. red = take; blue = bunt; green = swing away).

As the pitcher throws, the batter will pick up the color, identify the pitch, announce its corresponding action and react accordingly.

DRILL:
WEIGHT BACK

IMPROVES:
FOOTWORK

EXECUTION:

With a pitcher positioned about 20 feet away from the batter, instruct him to bounce a tennis ball to the hitter, so that the ball ends up in the strike zone.

Watch the ball out of the pitcher's hand, keep your weight back and load up to swing without lunging for the ball.

DRILL:
CHAIR DRILL

IMPROVES:
HANDS TO THE BALL

EXECUTION:

Place a chair in the batter's box, sit down and lock your ankles around the chair legs to anchor yourself in that position.

Wait for your partner to toss a ball into the strike zone.

Load up to swing using only your upper body.

Concentrate on bringing your hands through the zone without turning your wrists.

Your goal is to hit a line drive and finish the swing over your shoulder.

DRILL:
TAP

IMPROVES:
HANDS INSIDE THE BALL

EXECUTION:

Enlist a partner to toss balls to you from a kneeling position, in similar fashion to the soft-toss drill.

Rotate your rear hip toward the tossed ball, incorporating your lower body into the swing to generate power.

Move toward the ball as if you are going to hit it, but do not actually swing the bat. Instead, take the knob of the bat to the ball and simply tap it. Your hands have not committed to the pitch, but you are now in good position to keep your hands inside the ball if you were to complete your swing.

DRILL:
ON A ROLL

IMPROVES:
ACTIVE HANDS, CONSISTENT CONTACT

EXECUTION:

With a pitcher positioned behind a screen about 10 feet from home plate, set up in the batter's box on your knees.

Start your swing as the pitcher rolls the ball to you on the ground, leading the knob of the bat with your bottom hand, following with the head of the bat led by your top hand and striking the ball.

If your bat strikes the ground, make necessary adjustments to level your swing, hitting the center of the ball and generating a low line drive back to the pitcher.

DRILL:
PLATE DISCIPLINE

IMPROVES:
HITTING FOR DIFFERENT COUNTS

EXECUTION:

Set up a tee atop home plate.

Adjust the tee to the position of your ideal pitch, one you would like to hit when you're ahead in the count, and take several swings.

Move the tee to a location beyond this ideal spot in both directions and take more swings to determine your range, which is your zero-strike hitting zone.

Move the tee again to several locations just outside of the zero-strike zone to determine your one-strike zone.

Move the tee even further to work on hitting pitches that are too close to take with two strikes.

DRILL:
FENCE DRILL

IMPROVES:
SHORT, QUICK SWING

EXECUTION:

Set up in your stance parallel to a fence and less than one bat length away from it.

Envision an inside pitch and swing your bat. Don't hit the fence.

Make sure to open your hips and get your hands out in front. Drag your bat head through the zone and extend it toward the imaginary ball. Do not loop the bat as you swing.

DRILL:
POWER BAT

IMPROVES:
ACCELERATION OF SWING

EXECUTION:

Set up in your batting stance next to a tee.

Instead of a baseball, place a soccer ball or basketball atop the tee. (If the tee does not support the weight of the ball, place a clean plunger upside-down into the tee so that the ball can rest in its wide base.)

Execute your normal swing, making sure not to decelerate when you make contact with the ball, which will be much heavier than a baseball. Retain a powerful swing until you follow through.

DRILL:
INSIDE, OUTSIDE

IMPROVES:
REACTING TO PITCHES, STRIDE

EXECUTION:

Set up two tees – one in front of the plate on the inside corner and the other in the middle of the plate on the outside corner. The tee in front of the plate should be set at a lower height than the outside tee.

Place a ball on each tee and stand back while you set up in your stance.

As you begin your stride, have someone else call out "inside" or "outside."

Adjust your swing to hit the appropriate ball.

DRILL:

IN, OUT, UP THE MIDDLE

IMPROVES:

DRIVING THE BALL TO ALL FIELDS

EXECUTION:

Place two cones on the edge of the outfield grass, one behind the shortstop and one behind the second baseman, dividing the field into three regions.

Place two strips of colored tape from the front to the back of home plate, dividing the plate into three regions, as well.

Take batting practice as usual. As each pitch approaches the plate, announce its location (inside, outside, middle) and make an adjustment to hit the ball to the appropriate region of the field.

DRILL:

SACRIFICE TARGET GAME

IMPROVES:

BUNT PLACEMENT

EXECUTION:

With four players – a pitcher, hitter, third baseman and first baseman – positioned on the field, place two cones halfway between home and first and another two cones between home and third to act as targets for the player who is bunting.

Set up in your stance and attempt to bunt each pitch as it is thrown; you do not have to bunt a bad pitch.

Each bunt that goes between the cones on either side is worth one point. After 10 pitches, rotate one position in the field until each of your teammates has bunted.

DRILL:

RELAY (THROWS) RACE

IMPROVES:

FOOTWORK, QUICK TRANSFER

EXECUTION:

Assemble two equal lines of players, spaced at intervals.

Begin with the ball on the same end of each line of players.

On the signal, catch the ball from the previous player in line, focusing on receiving the ball, pivoting and making an accurate throw to the next player.

Once the ball has reached the last player, he will throw "through" the cutoffs and back to the first player in line. The winning team is the first to complete the relay throws.

DRILL:
BARE-HANDED DOUBLE PLAYS

IMPROVES:
RECEIVING AND TRANSFERRING THE BALL

EXECUTION:

With a second baseman and shortstop in their normal positions and without gloves, a coach should alternate rolling ground balls to each player.

The player receiving the ball should concentrate on fielding with both hands and making an accurate throw to second base.

The player not fielding the ball should cover the bag, catching the ball with both hands and completing the double play with a throw to first.

DRILL:
SHALLOW FLY BALLS

IMPROVES:
TAGGING UP, JUDGMENT

EXECUTION:

Line up as a runner at third base.

Have a teammate or coach hit shallow fly balls to the outfield.

Read the fly ball off the bat and determine whether the ball will be caught and whether you should tag up.

If the ball will be caught, go back to the bag and get set to take off for home, leaving third base as soon as the ball hits the fielder's glove.

DRILL:
PITCH TRAJECTORY

IMPROVES:
READING PITCHES

EXECUTION:

Start with a runner on first base, but vary the situation by changing the number of runners throughout the drill.

A coach should throw pitches to a catcher, with some landing in the dirt.

As a runner, watch the coach's delivery to determine if the ball will be in the dirt. With a runner on first only, steal without hesitation when you determine that the ball will be in the dirt. With runners on second and third, work on taking an aggressive secondary lead when the ball is in the dirt.

DRILL:
BEAT THE BALL

IMPROVES:
SPEED

EXECUTION:

Set up in a normal defense.

Soft-toss a ball to a hitter so that he can hit the ball in play.

The hitter becomes the base runner, attempting to round the bases before the defense fields the ball and throws to first base, second base, third base and home.

Practice making good turns by pushing off the inside of each bag.

DRILL:
SWAY AND FRAME

IMPROVES:
JUDGMENT ON FRAMING PITCHES

EXECUTION:

A coach begins the first round by throwing five pitches to the catcher.

React to each pitch, and, if needed, catch the ball and determine whether or not to frame the pitch.

Acting as an umpire, the coach determines if the catcher made the correct decision.

If the catcher is correct, the coach proceeds to the next round, decreasing the number of pitches thrown by one; if the catcher is incorrect, he returns all balls to the coach, and the round is repeated.

Your goal is to complete five rounds without returning any balls.

DRILL:
CAUGHT STEALING

IMPROVES:
QUICK RELEASE, THROWING ACCURACY

EXECUTION:

After a pitcher simulates a pitch and a runner simulates a steal attempt from first, receive the pitch and make a throw to second.

A coach times the catcher with a stopwatch as he makes the throw, stopping the watch once the tag has been applied to the runner.

Repeat and attempt to improve your time.

DRILL:
GOALIE

IMPROVES:
BLOCKING PITCHES IN THE DIRT

EXECUTION:

Place a cone on each side of the catcher. Vary the cones' width depending on age and skill level.

A coach should position himself about 30 feet away from the catcher.

The coach throws balls to the catcher between the cones, varying pitches thrown in the air and in the dirt to ensure that the catcher isn't dropping too early.

The throws should vary on each side and in front of the catcher. Track the number of "goals" that the catcher allows through the cones.

Repeat the drill until you allow very few "goals," then widen the distance between cones to test your range.

DRILL:
RELAY GROUND BALL

IMPROVES:
FIELDING TECHNIQUE

EXECUTION:

Place a cone in the baseline between second and third base. Set up between the cone and second base in the ready position.

A partner or coach should roll a ground ball close to the cone or farther to your right.

If the ball is close to the cone, get behind it to make the play.

If the ball is far to your right, backhand the ball.

As you master both plays, extend the distance between the cone and the base.

DRILL:
PEPPER

IMPROVES:
SOFT HANDS, KEEPING THE BALL IN FRONT

EXECUTION:

One player hits light, check-swing ground balls to a line of fielders who are standing about 15 feet away. Use a tennis ball.

You should try to field the ball and soft-toss it back to the batter as quickly as possible.

When you make an error, you are out. The last man standing wins.

Once you master it with gloves, try pepper bare-handed.

DRILL:
STAR

IMPROVES:
CATCHING, THROWING

EXECUTION:

Have a coach hit a ground ball to the shortstop, who throws the ball to the first baseman, who throws to the second baseman, who throws to the third baseman, who throws to the catcher at home.

Follow your throw, assuming the position of the base to which you have thrown, with the catcher moving to shortstop.

When receiving the ball, place a tag on the base before making the next throw.

DRILL:
QUARTERBACK DRILL

IMPROVES:
FIELDING LONG FLY BALLS

EXECUTION:

A coach should begin in a position about 10 feet in front of an outfielder.

With the ball in his hand, he will point in the direction of the player's first step.

Take a drop step in that direction and continue running on an angle until the coach points in another direction.

Plant your outside leg and step with your inside leg to change directions, keeping your eyes on the coach throughout the drill.

After several changes in direction, the coach will throw the ball. Position yourself to get under the ball and make the catch.

DRILL:
GET THE ANGLE

IMPROVES:
FIELDING BALLS IN THE GAP

EXECUTION:

Assume a position in the outfield as a coach throws balls on the ground and in the air to simulate different outfield hits.

Take an angle to the ball, making sure you get behind it to make the play so that you field the ball with your momentum coming toward the infield.

Your goal is to keep the ball in front of you at all times and not to let it get past.

DRILL:
COMBINATION DRILL

IMPROVES:
POSITIONING, FOOTWORK, THROWING, HITTING THE CUTOFF

EXECUTION:

The drill begins with a catcher, a shortstop acting as the cutoff man and an outfielder.

A coach hits a fly ball to the outfielder, who catches it and throws to the cutoff man.

As you are throwing, the coach should hit a short fly ball to you so that you must run forward to make the catch and again throw to the cutoff man.

Continue to run toward the infield, getting in proper position to catch a line drive hit by the coach. Throw to either the catcher or the cutoff, depending on your position on the field.

The coach will continue to hit balls to you, but now you're on the infield. This continues until you are close enough to place the ball into the catcher's glove without making a throw.

SOURCE NOTES

TOP ONE: BASIC FUNDAMENTALS

Page 22: Schilling quote: Kenda, Rich. "Focusing and Long Toss Key Pitching Success." *USA Today Baseball Weekly.* March 19, 2002.

TOP THREE: PITCHING – MECHANICS

Page 78: Mazzone quote: Mazzone, Leo with Jim Rosenthal. *Pitch Like a Pro.* New York, N.Y.: St. Martin's Press. 1999. p. 39.

Page 78: Seaver quote: Schlossberg, Dan. *Pitching: An Official Major League Baseball Book.* New York, N.Y.: Simon & Schuster. 1991. p. 20.

Page 80: Dr. Andrews reference: Hyman, Mark. "A Children's Crusade." *Sports Illustrated.* June 7, 2010. p. 18–19.

BOTTOM THREE: PITCHING – COMMAND

Page 96: Drysdale, Spahn quotes: Schlossberg, Dan. *Pitching: An Official Major League Baseball Book.* New York, N.Y.: Simon & Schuster. 1991. p. 46.

Page 96: Marsh quote: Williams, Pete. "The Umpires: Zoned Out – or on the Ball." *USA Today Baseball Weekly.* April 15, 1998.

Page 98: Anderson reference, Biggio quote: Williams, Pete. "Rollerblade Gear Pads Hitters' Stats." *USA Today Baseball Weekly.* August 19, 1998. p. 5.

Page 99: Glavine quote: Williams, Pete. "The Pitching Prankster." *USA Today Baseball Weekly.* August 20, 1997. p. 12.

Page 103: Wohlers quote: Mazzone, Leo with Jim Rosenthal. *Pitch Like a Pro.* New York, N.Y.: St. Martin's Press. 1999. p. 55.

Page 108: Pettitte quote: Kenda, Rich. "Instructional Series: How to Hold Baserunners Close." *USA Today Baseball Weekly.* June 13, 2001.

TOP FOUR: PITCHING – HEAT

Page 114: Schilling quotes: Williams, Pete. "Power Profile: Curt Schilling." *Mind & Muscle Power Magazine.* September 2000. p. 60.

Page 117: Seaver quote: Seaver, Tom with Lee Lowenfish. *The Art of Pitching.* New York, N.Y.: Mountain Lion Books. 1984. p. 94.

Page 120: Lincecum quote: Verducci, Tom. "How Tiny Tim Became a Pitching Giant." *Sports Illustrated.* July 7, 2008.

Page 125: Clemens quotes: Williams, Pete. "Power Pitcher – Leg Strength Gives This Yankee His Leading Edge." *Muscular Development.* July 1999. p. 108–112.

BOTTOM FOUR: HITTING – APPROACH

Page 128: Bagwell, Gwynn reference: Verducci, Tom. "One of a Kind." *Sports Illustrated.* July 19, 1999.

TOP FIVE: HITTING – CONTACT

Page 144: Gammons reference: Gammons, Peter. "A Real Rap Session." *Sports Illustrated.* April 14, 1986.

Page 153: La Russa quote: Barrow, Eric. "Stroke of Genius." New York *Daily News.* July 8, 2007.

BOTTOM FIVE: HITTING – POWER

Page 160: Gwynn quote: Williams, Pete. "Learning to 'Let It Go' Gwynn Has Best Season." *USA Today Baseball Weekly.* September 10, 1997. p. 6.

Page 164: Delgado quote: Krasner, Steven. *Play Ball Like the Pros.* Atlanta, Ga.: Peachtree Publishers. 2002. p. 146.

TOP SIX: COACHING TIPS

Page 176: Ripken reference: Ripken, Cal Jr. and Bill with Larry Burke. *Play Baseball the Ripken Way.* New York, N.Y.: Random House. 2004. p. 11.

Page 177: Carew quote: Williams, Pete. "Young and Talented Angels are Submitting to a Higher Calling." *USA Today Baseball Weekly.* August 12–22, 1995. p. 32–33.

Page 186: Marsh, DeMuth, La Russa references: Williams, Pete. "Umpires' Images Takes a Beating With New Stresses." *USA Today Baseball Weekly.* March 10, 1993. p. 26.

Page 189: Gwynn reference: Williams, Pete. "Gwynn's Big Reason to Grin." *USA Today Baseball Weekly.* March 5, 1997. p. 8.

BOTTOM SIX: ADVANCED FUNDAMENTALS

Page 193: Pierre, Butler quotes: Curry, Jack. "The Lost Art: Strategy of the Bunt; No More Easy Outs." *The New York Times.* August 17, 2003.

Page 194: Alomar quote: Kenda, Rich. "Instructional Series: Bunting: The Supreme Sacrifice." *USA Today Baseball Weekly.* June 24, 1998.

TOP SEVEN: BASERUNNING

Page 208: Zimmer on Fisk: Kurkjian, Tim. "Basepaths belong to Jeter." ESPN.com. January 19, 2005.

BOTTOM SEVEN: FIELDING – CATCHERS

Page 225: Bench quote: Bench, Johnny with Paul Daugherty. *Catch Every Ball: How to Handle Life's Pitches.* Wilmington, Ohio: Orange Frazer Press. 2008.

Page 225: Berra quote: Berra, Yogi. "Catching Perfection." *The New York Times.* May 22, 1998.

TOP EIGHT: FIELDING – INFIELDERS

Page 242: Gillick quote: Will, George F. *Men at Work: The Craft of Baseball.* New York, N.Y.: Macmillan Publishing Co. 1990. p. 232.

Page 242: Smith quote: Smith, Ozzie with Rob Rains. *Ozzie Smith: The Road to Cooperstown.* Canada: Sports Publishing L.L.C. 2002.

Page 244: Alomar quote: Verstegen, Mark and Pete Williams. *Core Performance.* New York, N.Y.: Rodale Press. 2004. p. 95.

Page 244: Garciaparra quote: Williams, Pete. "The Power of Glove." *USA Today Baseball Weekly.* August 12, 1998. p. 8–9.

BOTTOM EIGHT: FIELDING – OUTFIELDERS

Page 264: Damon quote: Kenda, Rich. "Instructional Series: Throwing Mechanics." *USA Today Baseball Weekly.* May 15, 2001.

TOP NINE: RULE BOOK BASICS

Page 282: Layne quote: "Ask the Umpire." MLB.com. July 13, 2010.

PHOTO CREDITS

RICH PILLING: Cover, 4–7, 20–21, 26–27 (Gwynn Jr., Hairston), 47, 49 (Bat rack), 52 (Chavez), 58 (Sanchez), 65 (Pierre), 67, 74, 81, 86, 90–91, 103, 114–115, 124, 131 (Bagwell), 134–135, 138–139, 145, 150 (Bagwell), 157, 158–159, 168, 180, 186–187, 192, 200, 202, 204–205, 214–215, 216–217, 218 (Utley), 228, 236–237, 244–245 (Longoria, Fielder), 253, 264–265 (Fielder), 266–270, 293 (Crawford), 295, 299 (Sabathia), 305 (Zimmerman)

TREVOR BROWN JR./RICHARD CLARKSON AND ASSOCIATES, LLC: 2–3

JONATHAN DANIEL/GETTY IMAGES: 12–13, 22, 63 (Royals), 118, 163 184 (Keppinger), 258–259

STEPHEN DUNN/GETTY IMAGES: 15 (Ramirez), 69 (Angels), 141, 150 (Lowrie), 154, 185 (Francona)

JARED WICKERHAM/GETTY IMAGES: 15 (Jeter), 184 (Strasburg), 261

GREGORY SHAMUS/GETTY IMAGES: 15 (Shin-Soo Choo)

DILIP VISHWANAT/GETTY IMAGES: 16 (Kouzmanoff), 20 (Pujols), 106, 167 (Pujols)

ERIK RANK/MLB PHOTOS: 17 (Grip), 24, 79 (Grip), 80, 84, 87, 130–131, 146, 148 (Swing) 170, 194–195, 210–213, 229, 232, 280–281

BOB LEVEY/GETTY IMAGES: 18 (Hernandez)

J. MERIC/GETTY IMAGES: 18 (Encarnacion), 23, 129 (Batting Grip), 252

OTTO GREULE JR./GETTY IMAGES: 19, 107 (Aardsma), 131 (Thomas), 140, 149, 166, 167 (Ortiz), 184 (Black), 185 (Cantu), 198, 240–241, 254, 262–263

JIM McISAAC/GETTY IMAGES: 25, 60–61, 63 (Yankees), 148 (Jeter), 152, 171 (Victorino), 227, 272–273

AL BELLO/GETTY IMAGES: 26 (Rodriguez), 289

GREG FIUME/GETTY IMAGES: 27 (Jones), 255

JONATHAN WILLEY/MLB PHOTOS: 28–41

JAMIE SQUIRE/GETTY IMAGES: 42–43, 57, 174–175,

MIKE STOBE/GETTY IMAGES: 44–45

COURTESY OF LOUISVILLE SLUGGER: 48–49

MARK CUNNINGHAM/MLB PHOTOS: 50, 53 (Shin-Soo Choo), 181, 209

COURTESY OF WILSON: 51, 55 (Mask, Chest Protector), 59

COURTESY OF FRANKLIN: 51 (Batting Glove)

COURTESY OF RAWLINGS: 53

HARRY HOW/GETTY IMAGES: 54

MICHAEL ZAGARIS/MLB PHOTOS: 55 (Fox), 188, 306

JED JACOBSOHN/GETTY IMAGES: 56, 68, 126–127, 250, 274–275, 278, 305 (Karros)

COURTESY OF NIKE: 58

SCOTT D. WEAVER/MLB PHOTOS: 59 (Cruz)

CHRISTIAN PETERSEN/GETTY IMAGES: 64, 108, 183, 265, 299 (Upton)

AL MESSERSCHMIDT/GETTY IMAGES: 65 (Damon), 109

JIM ROGASH/GETTY IMAGES: 66, 82–83, 172

KEVORK DJANSEZIAN/GETTY IMAGES: 69 (Matsui)

EZRA SHAW/GETTY IMAGES: 70 (Yankees), 71, 219, 249, 277, 298 (Crisp), 302

MARC SEROTA/GETTY IMAGES: 70 (Cardinals), 167 (Delgado)

ELSA/GETTY IMAGES: 73, 179

SCOTT CUNNINGHAM/GETTY IMAGES: 75

BRIAN BAHR/GETTY IMAGES: 76–77, 300 (Gonzalez)

RON VESELY/MLB PHOTOS: 79 (Buehrle), 92–93, 100–101, 193, 218 (Fontenot), 256, 283, 287

HARRY HOW/GETTY IMAGES: 79 (Nomo), 121

JOHN WILLIAMSON/MLB PHOTOS: 85, 99, 147, 218 (Upton), 234–235, 251

DREW HALLOWELL/GETTY IMAGES: 88–89

MATTHEW STOCKMAN/GETTY IMAGES: 96–97

RICK STEWART/GETTY IMAGES: 97

LOUIS REQUENA/MLB PHOTOS: 98, 116

ANDY LYONS/GETTY IMAGES: 102

POUYA DIANAT/ATLANTA BRAVES/MLB PHOTOS: 104

CHRIS HAMILTON/MLB PHOTOS: 105

DOUG PENSINGER/GETTY IMAGES: 107 (Burke), 132, 156

BRAD MANGIN/MLB PHOTOS: 107 (Morneau), 110–111, 113 (Lincecum), 129 (Teixeira), 133, 169, 176, 197, 222–223, 226, 246–247, 257, 294, 297, 300 (Litsch)

BUD SYMES/GETTY IMAGES: 113 (Ryan)

KEVIN C. COX: GETTY IMAGES: 113 (Wagner), 248, 265 (Heyward), 271, 293 (Heyward), 303 (McCann), 304, 305 (Longoria)

MLB PHOTOS: 119, 161, 203, 220, 301

JOHN GRIESHOP/MLB PHOTOS: 122–123, 151, 182, 244 (Pujols), 286

BRUCE KLUCKHOHN/GETTY IMAGES: 136

LEON HALIP/GETTY IMAGES: 142–143, 155 (Cabrera)

NICK LAHAM/GETTY IMAGES: 150 (Teixeira), 206–207, 284–285

HANNAH FOSLIEN/GETTY IMAGES: 155 (Jeter)

ELIOT J. SCHECHTER/GETTY IMAGES: 162

J.P. VERNI/MLB PHOTOS: 164–165

PAUL SPINELLI/MLB PHOTOS: 171 (Pedroia), 224, 230–231, 238–239

STEPHEN O'BRIEN/MLB PHOTOS: 190–191

NAM Y. HUH/AP PHOTO: 196

MICHAEL IVINS/BOSTON RED SOX/MLB PHOTOS: 218 (Youkilis)

JEFF GROSS/GETTY IMAGES: 233, 298 (Loney)

TOM PIGEON/GETTY IMAGES: 243

SARA WOLFRAM/GETTY IMAGES: 290–291

CHRISTOPHER RUPPEL/GETTY IMAGES: 296

RONALD MARTINEZ/GETTY IMAGES: 303 (Patterson)